THE INCLUSIVE LANGUAGE HANDBOOK

THE
INCLUSIVE
LANGUAGE
HANDBOOK

A Guide to
Better Communication and
Transformational Leadership

JACKIE FERGUSON
ROXANNE BELLAMY

the
diversity
movement

Please note: Inclusive language is constantly evolving. This handbook
details current best practices at the time of publication, but the terms we
suggest and the contexts around them will certainly change over time.
The Diversity Movement will update and revise this book and the specific
words we recommend to honor people, their identities, and experiences.

As you read, it will be helpful to have a notebook or journal available
where you can take notes and complete the handbook exercises.

ISBN: 978-0-578-29160-4

The Diversity Movement
4801 Glenwood Avenue
Raleigh, NC 27612

This book, like so many things we do, is dedicated to our children, Diana and Killian, who will live, love, and lead in a more inclusive world.

Contents

SPECIFIC INDUSTRY GUIDANCE

REVIEW, REFLECTION, AND NEXT STEPS

SUPPLEMENTARY INFORMATION

WHAT THIS BOOK TEACHES

How you communicate is critical to the way you are perceived, how you make other people feel, and the culture you create.

Have you ever felt excluded, offended, or misunderstood because of a word or a phrase that someone used? Have you ever felt uncomfortable—or at a loss for what to say—when talking about some aspect of personal identity? If so, you're not alone.

It can be hard to know how to communicate appropriately, both in our personal lives and in the workplace. Sometimes it's challenging to know what language to avoid and, at other times, what language is the most respectful. In our ever-evolving society, how people describe themselves is always changing too. But one thing is certain:

No matter who you are or the work you do, your word choice matters.
Thoughtfully chosen words can be powerful relationship builders, while ill-chosen or unthinking comments can alienate and offend. In the workplace specifically, repeating harmful language over time creates a toxic company culture, high employee turnover, and a damaged reputation.

The *Inclusive Language Handbook* is designed to help you get comfortable discussing all aspects of human diversity and identity. You'll learn how to consistently use respectful language that promotes inclusion, productivity, and teamwork. You'll discover professional best practices for choosing words that help every individual feel valued, supported, and motivated. Last but not least, you'll learn how to drive positive culture change by spreading the practice of inclusive language throughout your community and organization.

Three features set this handbook apart:

1. Context: Clear explanations of why inclusive language is needed and the benefits it delivers
2. Handbook exercises that provide valuable practice
3. Real-world insights and industry-specific guidance from organization leaders

Use this guide to:

- Explore the purpose, intention, and value of inclusive language
- Learn the six essential guidelines for inclusive language
- Avoid the pitfalls of offending others
- Discover best practices for inclusive language use
- Gain valuable practice communicating about diverse identities
- Explore how to build an inclusive company culture through respectful language

Get started today by improving your knowledge and ability to communicate inclusively. Practicing inclusive language will help your organization build and retain a diverse, productive, and loyal team. By committing to use these terms—and keep learning as terms evolve—you'll be rewarded with stronger, more trusting relationships, and a more respectful and enjoyable work environment. Your leadership as an inclusive communicator will help to build a healthy company culture where every person feels welcomed, accepted, and empowered to do their best work consistently.

WHAT'S IN A WORD?

In business, sometimes, even one unthinking word, unintentionally insulting phrase, or negative comment can be a game changer. It may make the difference between retaining a productive, loyal employee and beginning yet another expensive hiring search. It may derail your efforts to build a warm and trusting customer relationship and send a client to your competition instead.

Since launching The Diversity Movement, our most frequently downloaded piece of content—by a wide margin—has been our white paper on inclusive language, called "Say This, Not That." We know from experience that executives, managers, and frontline professionals across the globe are searching for just the right words to make people feel comfortable and engaged. Language use causes many people to get worried, anxious, confused, or even frustrated. But, we know you want to do better. Businesspeople recognize the reality that language can make their workplace culture welcoming and supportive or alienating, divisive, and potentially toxic.

That's why we've developed this handbook. It's designed to teach you inclusive language guidelines, best practices, and specific words and phrases that promote a productive workplace culture. It will show you how to make your language respectfully mirror how people talk about themselves.

Completing the exercises in this handbook will help you integrate inclusive language into every conversation, presentation, social media post, and email. It will raise your awareness and enhance the way you and your company do business.

In our increasingly diverse society, the words people use to describe themselves and their individual identities are evolving. As society changes, certain words and phrases may rapidly go in and out of favor. Return to credible resources frequently to stay up to date.

We advise our clients at The Diversity Movement that, if you take only one single action toward a more inclusive workplace, start by embracing the use of inclusive language. It's the spark that activates a culture of diversity, equity, and inclusion (DEI). And a culture of DEI has been proven to drive employee engagement, loyalty, productivity, and bottom-line results. But I'll be honest, once organizations take that first step, it almost always sparks the start of a DEI adventure.

Use this handbook to make inclusive language your daily practice. You'll clear the path for everyone in your organization to do their best work. We know from years of experience with hundreds of client organizations that practicing inclusive language will reward you, your colleagues, and your customers. As a matter of fact, inclusive language will strengthen and transform your entire company culture.

—**Jackie Ferguson**
Co-Founder and Head of Content and Programming, The Diversity Movement

INCLUSIVE LANGUAGE: AN INTRODUCTION

What Is Inclusive Language and Why Does It Matter?

Inclusive language is the daily practice of communicating intentionally using unbiased words that acknowledge diversity, convey respect, and support an environment of equitable opportunity.

The words "daily practice" are critical to this definition. Inclusive language is not simply an idea or an aspiration. It comes to life and generates impact only when it's routinely practiced in everyday workplace conversations and written communications.

Consistent use of inclusive language can have a significant, positive effect on a company's culture, performance, and profitability. Why? Because language shapes human relationships, and **people are at the heart of organizations**. Using inclusive language honors each person's diverse identity, making them feel welcomed, valued, and empowered to do their best work. Productive collaboration is driven by inclusive communication, as is teamwork and trust.

By contrast, using exclusive, insensitive, or discriminatory language can cause tangible harm to people and organizations, including:

- Damaged relationships
- Alienation
- Inaccurate perceptions of values and beliefs
- Diminished productivity and engagement
- Reduced innovation
- Lower quality problem-solving
- Higher turnover rates

Sometimes, it's the small patterns of our daily lives that subtly reinforce exclusion and discrimination. Practicing inclusive language helps to reduce or eliminate microaggressions (that is, spur-of-the-moment, offhand comments about personal identity that insult or belittle others). These all-too-common, subtle acts of exclusion and rejection—even when unintended—are known to have a cumulative negative effect on employee mental health, productivity, and problem-solving capacity. Whether these slights, snubs, and insults are inadvertent, or they stem from the speaker's unexamined linguistic habits, or are steeped in deeper prejudice, they understandably contribute to a sense of inequality in a corporate culture.

On sites such as Glassdoor, Comparably, and LinkedIn, there is a growing tide of employee-generated ratings and reviews of employer promises and policies related to diversity, equity, and inclusion. This real-world feedback confirms that noninclusive language damages employer–employee relationships. When employees feel defined by their otherness, excluded from a majority-defined workplace culture, or believe their perspectives are not welcome, they are less likely to contribute ideas or do great work. Also, disgruntled employees are likely to tell others about their displeasure as they search for employment somewhere else.

No one can do their best work or be their full, authentic self in a place where they don't feel welcome. Employees won't stay long if they feel their company has a toxic culture that doesn't value and respect them. And turnover is expensive. In fact, the average cost to replace an employee is roughly 50% of that employee's annual salary but can be as high as 150%.[1]

For companies that don't embrace inclusive language, the downside risks are clear. What may be less obvious are the impressive and inspiring upside benefits to organizations that communicate inclusively. The fact is, practicing inclusive language is one of the most powerful tools a company can employ to recruit, hire, and retain a diverse workforce. A decade of research into successful business practices reveals a significant correlation between diversity and high-performing organizations. A diverse work environment fosters innovation, increases revenue, and improves decision-making results.

- According to the Forbes Insights Report "Fostering Innovation Through a Diverse Workforce," 85% of today's employees believe that "a diverse and inclusive workforce is crucial to encouraging different perspectives and ideas that drive innovation."[2]
- For every 10% more racially or ethnically diverse a company's senior team is, earnings before interest and taxes (EBIT) are nearly 1% higher.[3]
- Companies with the most ethnically diverse executive teams—not only with respect to absolute representation, but also with a variety or mix of ethnicities—are 33% more likely to outperform their peers on profitability, says McKinsey and Company.[4]

- Gender diversity contributes a similar advantage. According to the same 2018 McKinsey report, companies in the top 25th percentile for gender diversity on their executive teams are 21% more likely to experience above-average profitability.
- Companies that report above-average diversity on their management teams also report innovation revenue that is 19 percentage points higher than that of companies with below-average leadership diversity, according to a 2018 Boston Consulting Group study.[5]
- Diverse teams make better business decisions. "They bring more perspectives, experience, and information, which helps to reduce cognitive biases and improves accountability. [. . .] In fact, the most diverse teams made better decisions 87% of the time."[6]

Keep in mind that "diversity" includes not only the traditional, big-three dimensions of race, ethnicity, and gender identity, but also characteristics such as age, disability, education, sexual orientation, neurodiversity, and more. Building a workforce that is diverse in multiple ways generates broadly contrasting viewpoints. This drives more-creative problem-solving, decision-making, and innovation. It creates an inclusive culture where all contributors are welcome, and the best ideas win.

The Challenge: Integrating Inclusion with Diversity and Equity

Inclusive language is a powerful force for good, but words alone won't make a company great. Organizations need to walk their talk. All three elements of DEI—diversity, equity, and inclusion—inform and reinforce one another, creating a strong, stable triangle. The highest performing companies focus on inclusion in concert with diversity and equity. For this reason, before we delve further into the specific topic of inclusive language, it's important first to see where it fits into the larger DEI picture.

Diversity without Inclusion: Missing the Benefits

Some companies hire a diverse team but fail to establish an inclusive mode of communicating and collaborating. A variety of viewpoints may be on the table, but not all voices are heard, which quashes the benefits of having the valuable mix of perspectives the company worked so hard to create. As Nick Otto writes in *Employee Benefit News*, "while hiring and selection are important, oftentimes organizations place more emphasis on finding the people who fit the workplace as opposed to shaping the workplace to fit the best people."[7]

In other words, these companies ask their diverse employees to "fit in" rather than to bring their unique points of view to the discussion. Today's employees want to work in an accessible environment that welcomes each person's perspective. They want not only diversity, but also inclusion. To activate the benefits of workplace diversity, companies must cultivate a culture of inclusion.

Diversity and Inclusion without Equity: A Promise Unfulfilled

Some organizations hire a diverse team and commit to inclusion but fail to provide equitable opportunities for training, job positions, and advancement. These companies are likewise sabotaging their own potential success. A company with a culture of diversity and inclusion, but without equity, is offering its employees an empty career promise. If you want employees to stay loyal to your organization and grow into leaders over time, equity is essential to the strength of the DEI triangle.

The Integration Challenge

The challenge is how to put the power of all three elements of DEI to work within your organization simultaneously. In some ways, fostering the first two attributes, diversity and equity, is easier than creating a culture of inclusion. Why? Because diversity and equity can be initiated at the leadership level.

Executives can define organization-wide values, policies, and procedures and assign managers to implement them, but a culture of inclusion depends on the dozens of daily practices, customs, and habits of every individual in the company. It relies on human behavior. It can be hard for people to change the small patterns of their daily lives that may subtly reinforce exclusion and discrimination.

Let's look next at how practicing inclusive language can help your organization to meet this challenge, integrate all three components of DEI, and develop a culture of inclusion.

The Solution: Putting Inclusive Language into Practice

A helpful starting point for changing how we communicate is to examine our natural human tendencies and patterns.

Our Natural Communication Tendencies

It's human nature to organize and categorize our social world. Our brains are always seeking the most efficient way to process information, which means we often take shortcuts to categorize concepts. This includes the words and phrases we use to describe personal identity. Each person also holds a unique set of innate and sometimes automatic beliefs about various social groups based on family views, personal experiences, media messaging, and social group perspectives. These are called our unconscious biases.

Although forming these biases may be natural, they are often uninformed, unfair, or simply wrong because unconscious biases rely on social stereotypes. Unconscious biases are also often centered around perceived in-group/out-group identities. An in-group is a social group with which someone identifies, and an out-group is one with which they do not. In-group/out-group thinking is also natural and stems from our inherent tendency to organize the world. However, we run into problems when we start to rank our in-groups and out-groups as superior or inferior to each other.

How Inclusive Language Changes Our Patterns

Inclusive language asks us to examine our own unconscious biases, in-groups, and out-groups, then pay attention to our linguistic habits around them. This effort calls for thoughtfulness and personal growth, so we avoid reinforcing assumptions and harmful language about norms.

Inclusive language also combats the slights to others that occur in moments of unintentional word choice. These casual comments about personal identity—known as microaggressions—often undercut and insult others, and they contribute to a sense of inequality among coworkers. Subtle acts of exclusion, whether steeped in deeper prejudices or not, pervade our culture and often reveal our unexamined, unconscious biases. Although they may seem small, microaggressions have a cumulative effect on employee mental health, productivity, and problem-solving. Microaggressions may also create feelings of hostility and discrimination.

Inclusive language, on the other hand, helps to create workplace culture that feels safe, encouraging, and openly accessible. It welcomes and respects all forms of personal identity and the intersectionality between them—that is, the unique combinations of ways that people belong to multiple social categories at the same time, including race, class, gender, and sexual orientation. These kinds of social categorizations are often tied to overlapping, interdependent systems of discrimination or disadvantage in our society. For example, a Black, gay woman will have a different experience than a White, heterosexual woman.

How Inclusive Language Changes Company Culture

It's natural for employees to want a culture that feels safe, encouraging, and accessible for everyone. Sometimes, however, their unthinking word choice gets in the way. Their language doesn't always reflect what they actually want or believe.

In the process of learning to communicate inclusively, people gain a better understanding of diversity and embrace the humanity of others. They come to reject the false construct of normality and deviation that's all too common in our society. This misguided model defines some people's identities or experiences as "normal," while defining others as inferior, subordinate, irregular, broken, or incomplete. The truth is people are people, in all their diversity. There is no innate hierarchy between us and no such thing as "normal." When we accept these truths and begin to use intentional language to describe ourselves and others, we cultivate an inclusive company culture that celebrates, supports, and attracts people of diverse identities.

Effective Communication Drives High Performance

For any form of communication to be effective, it needs to address its intended audience appropriately. Inclusive language seeks to honor the diverse identity of each person in the room, inviting them to be part of the conversation.

These statistics illustrate the powerful, positive impact of effective communication in the workplace:

- Approximately 86% of employees and executives cite the lack of effective collaboration and communication as the two main causes of workplace failures. By contrast, teams that communicate effectively may increase their productivity by as much as 25%.[8]
- About 75% of employers rate teamwork and collaboration as "very important," yet only 18% of employees receive communication evaluations at their performance reviews.[9]
- Organizations that communicate effectively are 4.5 times more likely to retain the best employees.[10]
- Of employees who leave within the first year, 27% cite feeling "disconnected" to the organization.[11]
- Companies with strong cultures have seen a fourfold increase in revenue growth.[12]

Inclusive language may be just one brick in the effort to build an equitable culture, but it's the cornerstone. Inclusion fosters diversity. It welcomes and respects all forms of personal identity. Learning to communicate inclusively is one of the most powerful tools a company can employ to foster the development of a diverse and high-performing workforce.

By the Numbers: What Workers Are Experiencing

Up to now we've looked at inclusive language from the point of view of the communicator. It's also critical to consider communication from the viewpoint of the recipient/listener.

The following statistics provide a reality check on the most prevalent types of workplace discrimination experienced by today's employees. These findings make the case that DEI—and, more specifically, the practice of inclusive language—is sorely needed in the American workplace.

NEW STUDY: 3 in 5 U.S. employees have witnessed or experienced discrimination based on age, race, gender, or sexual orientation, according to the employee review platform, Glassdoor.[13]

Race/Ethnicity

Research conducted by the Society for Human Resource Management (SHRM)[14] showed vast disparities in the percentage of American workers who have felt unfairly treated in the workplace due to race or ethnicity over the last five years:

- Black 42%, Asian 26%, Hispanic/Latine 21%, White 12%
- Perceived sources of unfair treatment:
  - Leader/Manager (other than direct supervisor) 57%
  - Coworker 54%
  - Direct Manager/Supervisor 45%
  - Client or Customer 35%
  - Human Resources 23%

Other sources prove similar points: In a 2020 Gallup survey, 1 in 4 Black workers and 1 in 4 Hispanic workers said they have experienced discrimination at work in the last 12 months.[15]

And White Americans receive, on average, 36% more callbacks to interview than Black Americans with equal qualifications.[16]

Gender

- Only about 1 in 5 senior leaders is a woman, and 1 in 25 is a culturally diverse woman.[17]
- Women often face disrespectful and "othering" behavior in their workplaces. They are more likely than men to experience common microaggressions, including being interrupted or spoken over, having their judgment questioned, and being expected to speak on behalf of all people with their identity.[18]
- Nearly half (48.8%) of transgender employees reported experiencing discrimination (being fired or not hired) based on their gender status.[18]

Age[19]

- Among older employees, 60% have seen or experienced workplace age discrimination. Between 90% and 95% of those say it is common.
- Almost 25% of employees aged 45 and older have been subjected to negative comments about their age from supervisors or coworkers.
- Although older adults are brought in for interviews at a rate similar to younger applicants, older workers are offered jobs 40% less frequently than younger candidates with similar skills.
- Over 50% of coworkers who witnessed instances of age discrimination did not report it.

Sexual Orientation[20]

- 67.5% of LGBTQ+ employees reported that they have heard negative comments, slurs, or jokes about LGBTQ+ people at work.
- 46% of LGBTQ+ workers have experienced unfair treatment at work at some point in their lives, including being fired, not hired, or harassed because of their sexual orientation or gender identity.
- 50% of LGBTQ+ workers are not "out" to their current supervisor.
- 34% of LGBTQ+ employees have left a job due to treatment by their employer.

Religion

Regarding religion, 44% of Muslim people, 41% of Hindu people, and 30% of Jewish people report that they have experienced religious discrimination at work.[21]

Intersectional Identities

A 2019 Boston Consulting Group study shows the impact of intersectional identities on the feeling of workplace otherness. In this study, 74% of the control group defined as "White, heterosexual-cisgender men who are not veterans and who have no disability" feel that their perspectives are welcome and valued at work. However, respondents with just one dimension of diversity—for example, White females, racially diverse males, or veterans—were on average 4 to 6 percentage points less likely to feel included.[22]

Furthermore, the more dimensions of diversity that respondents reported, the less likely they were to feel included. People with three dimensions of diversity—queer women of color, for example—showed an even higher rate of feeling excluded. When employees feel defined by their otherness, feel excluded from a majority-defined workplace culture, or believe their perspectives are not welcome, they are less likely to contribute ideas, less likely to do great work, and more likely to look for employment elsewhere.

Where Is Your Company Today?

Before you begin your personal tutorial with this handbook, it's helpful to examine where your company stands today with regard to DEI in general, and inclusive language in particular. Completing this assessment will help you put the challenges that lie ahead into perspective and identify the best way forward in your workplace.

Maybe your company, like many others, is already focusing on DEI. Your organization has recognized the competitive advantage of workplace diversity. Your leadership team has read the statistics, articles, and comprehensive reports that urge them to engage in diverse hiring practices and to build an inclusive culture through empathetic, participative leadership. Your business has allocated necessary resources to diversify your team. Now you want to learn about inclusive language so you can better embrace the humanity of your colleagues.

Perhaps there are one or two departments or divisions within your company that are on board with DEI, but others are not. You're looking for ways to make your organization's values and practices more universal.

Or finally, maybe your team is not particularly diverse. You're at the DEI starting line. You might be a human resources professional who wants to begin writing inclusive job descriptions to attract diverse candidates. Or you may be a sales professional and find yourself pitching to increasingly diverse decision-makers. Perhaps you're an executive who needs to address a large group of people and ensure everyone in the room feels included. You're sensitive to the potential missteps of discriminatory language and want to avoid alienating others. You're searching for just the right things to say.

Whatever your particular role and your company's current DEI status, your personal commitment to learn and practice inclusive language will set a positive model for others to follow. However, keep in mind that everyone is responsible for an inclusive culture and for inclusive language use. Your colleagues need to join you in the practice in order for an organization-wide culture shift to occur.

The tutorial that follows will show you current best practices for inclusive workplace language. It will help you build the foundational skills required to confidently address any individual, or a room full of people with different identities, with empathy and humanity in mind.

HANDBOOK EXERCISES

TEN EFFECTIVE WAYS TO MEASURE DIVERSITY IN YOUR ORGANIZATION

For each of the following questions, choose an evaluative score between 0 and 10 that best reflects where you stand today. A score of 0 means no action/activity to date; 10 indicates ideal performance.

_____ We have analyzed the demographics of our employee population.

_____ We have researched the diversity of our market/geographic service area(s).

_____ The diversity of our leadership and employees mostly matches that of the customers and the communities we serve.

_____ Our senior leadership team consults with a diverse range of employees and/or advisors when setting policy and making substantive decisions.

_____ Our senior leadership team clearly communicates internally and externally that we are guided by the values of diversity, equity, and inclusion.

_____ We routinely offer voluntary diversity training to our employees.

_____ We have measured feelings of belonging and inclusion within our organization.

_____ We take the diversity of our employees and customers into account when designing processes, products, services, and communications.

_____ We actively explore opportunities to leverage diversity when launching new products/services and entering new markets.

_____ We routinely audit our DEI practices and results.

_____ /100

If you scored between:

0–50 ➜ Your company's DEI effort is in the design-and-build stage. Ensure you have established a strong foundation of enthusiastic leadership commitment to DEI values. Then, begin to develop a DEI action plan. A DEI consultant can provide valuable, time-saving assistance to help you define this plan.

51–80 ➜ Your company has established some key structural elements of DEI. This is a good stage to introduce voluntary, organization-wide DEI training on a regular basis. Focus on your categories with the lowest scores, identify roadblocks to progress, and start naming potential ways to move past them.

81–100 ➜ Congratulations on excellent progress so far. You are now in a position to explore effective ways to leverage your company's strengths in areas such as recruiting, employee retention, collaboration, customer relationship development, and new product/ market initiatives.

ADDITIONAL HANDBOOK EXERCISES

THE CONTEXT QUIZ
Make your best guess! Then, look for the answers at the end of this section.

1. What percentage of workers say inclusion efforts are important to them when choosing an employer?
2. What percentage of US companies have a DEI program already in place?
3. By what percent does customer satisfaction increase at companies that embrace inclusion and inclusive language?

IMAGINE THIS
You have a new supervisor at work. Your working relationship is getting off to a good start. He has invited you to join him for lunch at a nearby restaurant. During lunch he confides in you about the team members he feels will be best suited for an important upcoming assignment. He disparages two of your teammates based on factors that have nothing to do with their abilities—one who speaks with an accent, the other based on age. How do you imagine

you'd feel when hearing this? How would these comments impact your thoughts about your supervisor? And, what actions might you take in response—at lunch or afterward—with your supervisor and/or your teammates?

_____

_____

_____

UPON REFLECTION

Think about this: What are the three best actions your organization has implemented to strengthen DEI? And what do you think are the three best next steps your organization should take in the future? Write down your thoughts in brief bullet points.

_____

_____

_____

REAL-LIFE ASSIGNMENT

Ask a friend or relative if they have ever experienced comments at work that made them (or one of their coworkers) feel excluded or insulted. Ask how they handled it and what happened as a result.

_____

_____

_____

NEXT STEPS

Write down the number one thing that happened after you joined your current company that made you feel the most welcomed, included, and free to bring your best self to work. Ask three of your coworkers the same question. Record their answers too.

_____

_____

_____

THE CONTEXT QUIZ—ANSWERS

1. Among 1,300 respondents to a Deloitte survey 80% said inclusion efforts were an important factor when choosing a company.[23]

2. A recent survey by the Society for Human Resource Management, which tracked 84 different DEI practices, found that 32% of companies require some form of DEI training for employees and 34% offer training to managers. However:

   - 40% of companies view diversity work only as a way to mitigate legal, compliance, or reputational risks, with HR in an enforcer role.
   - 76% of companies have no diversity or inclusion goals.
   - 75% of companies do not have DEI included in the company's leadership development or overall learning and development curricula.[24]

3. Companies that embrace inclusion and inclusive language have 39% higher customer satisfaction, according to Deloitte.[25]

YOUR WORD-BY-WORD PRACTICAL TUTORIAL

Getting Started

Get Comfortable Being Uncomfortable

Even people who champion diversity and are knowledgeable about the topic can be nervous about choosing the correct words to describe various aspects of personal identity. This is especially true when interacting with people whose personal identities they have not often encountered. How should I address the chief marketing officer who identifies as a queer Black woman or the new administrative intern from Oman who uses a service animal at work? These moments put us face-to-face with our own insecurities, assumptions, and lack of awareness. They force us to reflect on our unconscious biases and linguistic habits.

To put it frankly, inclusive language doesn't often come naturally, even for people who believe in and advocate for the value of diversity. Using intentional, inclusive language requires us to continually examine our unconscious biases and linguistic customs. Learning to do it *well* requires education, mindfulness, and repetition. Practice helps us to avoid reinforcing harmful language habits and assumptions that can damage our relationships. Putting in the effort is well worth the potential results.

Progress, Not Perfection. Inclusive language, in its most fundamental form, focuses on understanding and embracing the humanity of communication. As you begin your inclusive language practice, remember that this is an ongoing journey with no finite destination. Learning to speak inclusively requires us to keep learning, practicing, and pushing ourselves toward personal growth.

You definitely won't get everything right at first. You'll hear yourself make mistakes. In those moments, especially as you think back about what you have learned from this handbook, you may feel embarrassed, frustrated, or discouraged. Remember that the first steps are always the hardest. Professional singers have vocal coaches and people across professions constantly need to upgrade or refresh their skills, so give yourself the space to learn without judgment.

Your increased sensitivity about language use is evidence that you are learning. It means you're starting down the right path. What's important is that you keep learning and trying. As long as you keep trying, you *will* make progress. Inclusive language is a lifelong practice— think of it as a kind of linguistic yoga. When you make a mistake, own it and apologize, correct it, then get back on track.

It's also worth noting that changing your language habits can feel like hard work. It might make you defensive, nervous, ashamed, confused, or bring up other emotions. All of those feelings are common and okay. What's important is that you take the first steps. Start learning and start practicing. *Get comfortable being uncomfortable.* Along the way, you will certainly make mistakes, but you will also find that people are forgiving when they know you are committed to being more inclusive.

Language is both a mirror and a force, constantly reflecting and influencing our actions, attitudes, and beliefs. That can be scary if you think that every word is a window to your unconscious bias, but each interaction can also be a window to your best intentions and personal growth.

If you build a diverse team and insist on inclusion, but then casually use insensitive terms that silently offend or discourage participation, you will have taken one step forward and two giant steps back. You know the risk of getting it wrong; this guide will show you how to get it right.

Ready to start? Here we go.

Six Guidelines for Inclusive Language

1. Put people first. Use person-first language. When describing others, start with the word "person" or "people." For example, say "a person with diabetes" versus "a diabetic." At first, this may seem like a minor or unnecessary distinction. It isn't. Adopting person-first language acknowledges the complexity of personal identity and recognizes that each person is so much more than any one of their identity descriptors. In other words, saying "a person with" maintains that the descriptor is just one aspect of that person's identity (just as you would say "a person who likes to cook" or "a person with brown hair"). Additionally, only include identity descriptors of people when they are relevant to the current discussion.

2. Use universal phrases. Avoid idioms, acronyms, jargon, and cultural phrases that may not make sense to all people. For instance, consider the American phrase "hit it out of the park," the British phrase "throw a spanner in the works," or the Australian phrase "it's chockers in here." All three are in English, yet none translates well outside of its native national culture. In a professional setting, phrases like these may impede effective communication and make people feel uncomfortable, embarrassed, confused, or excluded.

3. Recognize the impact of mental health language. When we describe everyday behaviors, moods, and personality characteristics using terms related to mental health diagnoses (for example, bipolar, PTSD, ADHD, or OCD), we minimize and deprecate the very real and serious impact these conditions have on people. Avoid using these terms unless they are medically diagnosed and shared with you personally. Even then, they probably won't be necessary or relevant to the conversation at hand. For the same reason, steer clear of derogatory terms that stem from the context of mental health such as schizo, spaz, paranoid, crazy, or psycho.

4. Use genderless language. Discontinue the generic use of "man" or "guy" to describe people, as in "mankind," "policeman," or "you guys." Those terms reinforce a culture that exclusively favors men. Replace these with terms that are gender-free, such as "humanity," "police officer," and "everyone." When choosing a pronoun for an unknown person, choose the singular "they," instead of "he" or the clunky "he/she." Doing so acknowledges the full spectrum of gender identities, including individuals who are nonbinary.

5. Be thoughtful about the imagery you use. Be sensitive in your use of symbolism. Take into consideration that some descriptors hold negative connotations for others and can therefore be offensive. Examples include the words "black," "dark," and "blind" as in "a black mark," "dark day," and "blind spot." Avoid this pitfall by expressing ideas literally when possible, for example, "It was a sad day," rather than, "It was a dark day."

6. Clarify if you aren't sure. As coworkers and customers get to know you better, they may choose to share aspects of their personal identity with you. Most people are happy to walk you through the language that makes them feel properly respected. Clarify with them if you're not sure. As you get to know others and feel comfortable with them, share your self-descriptors and pronouns. They are likely to share theirs with you too.

What to Say When You Don't Know What to Say

This section is *not* about how to make "small talk," how to get a discussion going, or how to be a witty conversationalist. It *is* about providing you with tools to speak inclusively and respectfully in the workplace, specifically regarding aspects of personal identity.

It's important to recognize up front that how we communicate at work is somewhat different from conversations in our personal lives. For a variety of reasons, the language we use at work needs to be well-considered, thoughtful, and intentional. Certainly, we're not suggesting or recommending that you speak carelessly, thoughtlessly, and hurtfully to others in your private life! But how you communicate in the workplace often has a ripple effect that goes far beyond the impact of personal conversations.

In addition, language usage at work sets the tone for your professional reputation. Thoughtful language use may help define how successful you are in collaborating with others and influence the productivity and success of your team, not to mention your company's culture. For all of these reasons, how you communicate in the workplace merits extra focus and attention. As an added bonus, your private conversations will benefit from inclusive language too.

In general, as you get to know people, pay attention to the terms and phrases they use to identify themselves. This is the heart of inclusive language practice. Your language should mirror their own. However, it's important not to generalize or assume. What you have learned about one person may not apply to everyone else. For example, even within the same family, one person may identify as Black, while another describes themselves as African American, or one person may use the term gay or lesbian, while another may identify as queer.

To speak inclusively, avoid generalizing. Remember that the notion that there is a "normal" majority—and that everyone else somehow isn't "normal"—is a false construct.

Let's look at some specific scenarios of what to say when you don't know what to say.

If you're unsure of how another person self-identifies, recognize that it is up to them whether, when, and how they wish to disclose this information. Over time, you will naturally tend to get to better know your coworkers and clients. Building close, trusting relationships and knowing a lot about each other can be a real benefit. However, you can still have a productive working relationship without knowing everyone's personal details. In fact, their personal details are usually irrelevant to their work.

Be sensitive to the fact that some people may feel uncomfortable or even fearful of the potential negative consequences of disclosing certain personal information, especially if you are working at companies or in communities that are not particularly diverse or inclusive. As a general rule, it's better to hold off on questioning others about their identity if it's not relevant to your conversation. Allow others to share with you over the course of time, as they are comfortable.

If a coworker or client asks you about some aspect of your personal identity, the tables are now turned. In this case, it's up to you to determine how to respond. You may be comfortable talking about aspects of your personal identity with others—for example, whether you are married, have children, have a disability, are a member of the LGBTQ+ community, are of mixed race, how old you are, and so forth. On the other hand, you may want to share these kinds of personal details only with people you know well. You might want to share certain aspects of your identity while keeping other parts private.

When you're new to an organization, it can be helpful to think through the kinds of questions you might be asked in advance and consider how you intend to respond. Decide what you're comfortable sharing and with whom. Assess how you want to phrase your responses. Doing this thinking in advance can help you avoid awkward pauses while keeping a positive working relationship with the questioner.

If you're ever caught off guard by a question that feels overly intrusive, you can always deflect it completely but diplomatically. Try saying "That's an interesting question, but first let me ask you about [insert neutral alternative topic here]." If you're asked a health or medical question that feels intrusive, try saying something like "I appreciate your concern, but I don't like to talk about medical topics at work. Thanks for understanding." These and similar answers are gentle ways to let the questioner know you'd like to maintain your privacy.

If you are asked by a coworker about some aspect of another person's identity, remember that this information is personal to the individual being discussed. Unless you know for certain that the person is open with everyone at work about that specific aspect of their identity, it's not your information to share. Instead, refer the questioner to the person they are asking about.

If you are writing someone's bio, introducing them at a large event, or describing them in an article, ask the individual how they wish to be described. Confirm what aspects of their personal identity, if any, they consider relevant to the context and want you to include.

To help you begin putting your new knowledge of inclusive language to work, we have organized the following tutorial based on seven individual identity categories. This information will make it easy for you to home in on specific topics.

Review these pages as needed to refresh your memory as you prepare for meetings, speaking engagements, or sales appointments with new accounts. You'll find best-practice inclusive language guidelines for:

1. Gender identity, sex, and sexuality
2. Disability and invisible illness
3. Mental, emotional, and cognitive diversity
4. Physicality
5. Cultural diversity: race, ethnicity, and nationality
6. Religion
7. Acquired diversity

Each section begins with an overview, general recommendations, and the reasoning and context for them. There is also a quick-reference table of specific suggestions for inclusive terminology. In the Reference section near the end of this handbook, you'll also find a list of colloquial expressions to avoid because of their discriminatory histories.

Seven Categories of Individual Identity

1 GENDER IDENTITY, SEX, AND SEXUALITY

As a first step, it's helpful to understand the differences between sex, gender, and sexual orientation. In short:

- **Sex** refers to a person's biological features or anatomy. It is typically classified as binary—female or male—although additional scientific research is revealing that sex is a spectrum, just like gender. In fact, current research suggests that up to 1.7% of the population is intersex, meaning they are born with biological characteristics that aren't 100% male or female.[26]

- **Gender** refers to social constructs and identities. Newborns are often assigned a gender (girl or boy) that matches their physical sex (male or female). People who continue to identify as the gender they were assigned at birth are referred to as cisgender. However, each person's gender is self-defined and can be changeable or even fluid. For some people, their biological sex doesn't match their gender identity. When a person's gender identity is opposite that of their biologically assigned sex, they might consider themselves transgender. Genders outside of the gender binary of man/woman include but are not limited to agender, gender queer, gender fluid, bigender, and gender variant.

- **Sexual orientation** refers to whom someone is sexually and/or romantically attracted to. Common sexual orientations include heterosexual, gay, lesbian, and bisexual. Queer is a broader term that can apply to both gender identity and sexual orientations including pansexual, asexual, and others.

Never presume to know a person's sex, gender identity, or sexual orientation based on their clothing, appearance, voice, or name. To understand how someone would like to be addressed, it's helpful to learn their pronouns (that is, the words they use in reference to themselves).

Common pronouns include she/her/hers, he/him/his, and they/them/theirs, but many others exist as well. If you don't know a person's pronouns, feel free to ask them and to share your own, but be careful to avoid the term "preferred pronouns" which implies that gender identity is a preference, not a fact. You might say something as simple as "Hi. I'm Sam. I use she/her pronouns. May I ask yours?"

As English speakers, when we select a pronoun, we are traditionally expected to choose a gender for the person we are referencing. For example, if we see someone walking down the hall and want to refer to them, we have to decide quickly which gender we think they might be. In that moment, without knowing the person at all, we often use their appearance to make an assumption. By doing so, we can unintentionally but easily misgender them based on social stereotypes. Misgendering is a common microaggression and can be intensely harmful to those who experience it repeatedly or intentionally.

Until recently, English offered no grammatically acceptable solution for referring to someone you don't know without using binary he/she pronouns. The best option for inclusive language was to insert the clunky—and still binary—phrases "he or she" or "him or her." This approach produced sentences like, "If an employee asks for my opinion, I will give it to him or her."

Thankfully, in recent years, English users have molded the language to be more inclusive and concise. Since 2019, all four of the major English language style guides—the Associated Press, the *Chicago Manual of Style*, the Modern Language Association's *MLA Style Manual*, and the *Publication Manual of the American Psychological Association*—accept the usage of singular "they." This means it is now grammatically correct to say "If an employee asks for my opinion, I will give it to them," even if you are only referring to one person. This is a great example of language as a living system. The singular *they* acknowledges and respects the wide range of diversity that exists in human sexuality, gender, and sexual orientation.

How we describe the range of diversity relating to gender, sex, and sexuality is also changing over time. For example, in the late 1980s, the acronym LGBT (standing for lesbian, gay, bisexual, and transgender) began making its way into mainstream vocabulary and served as a starting point for inclusion. Today, that acronym is sometimes expanded to LGBTQIAP+ —adding letters for queer, intersex, asexual, and pansexual, and a plus sign to signify other orientations, such as demisexual or Two-Spirit. Some people associate the Q with both queer and questioning. Some interpret the A as standing for both asexual and ally (an ally being an individual who does not personally belong to this group, but who supports human rights for people of all sexual orientations).

This wide variety of gender identities, sexual orientations, and evolving acronyms can definitely be challenging to keep up with, especially if you're new to inclusive language practice. With such a broad spectrum of identities to consider, how can you possibly know what to say? The important point to remember is to not make assumptions. Get to know people. Listen to how they refer to themselves. When you don't know what words to choose, ask others for guidance. Inclusive language isn't a trap that someone is attempting to trick you to fall into. People just want you to be empathetic and compassionate, so listening, learning, and asking are always the best default options.

Review the LGBTQ+ alphabet and inclusive language list here to learn more.

The LGBTQ+ Alphabet. Here is a partial list of common terms people may use for gender identity and sexual orientation.

- **Ally** refers to someone who shows allyship to the LGBTQ+ community. Being an ally is an ongoing and active process through which someone chooses to stand up for—and stand beside—marginalized or underrepresented communities by taking actions that improve belonging, dismantle barriers to inclusion, and challenge existing systems of exclusion or oppression.
- **Asexual** refers to someone who typically does not experience sexual attraction. This person can experience romantic attraction. The prefix "a" comes from ancient Greek and means "not" or "without"

- **Aromantic** refers to someone who has little or no romantic attraction to others. Aromantic individuals may be asexual or not.
- **Bi-curious** refers to someone who is exploring bisexuality but does not necessarily identify as bisexual.
- **Bisexual** refers to someone who is sexually attracted to more than one gender. This often means being attracted to both men and women (the traditional binary genders), hence the "bi" prefix.
- **Cisgender** refers to a person whose gender identity corresponds with the physical sex they were assigned at birth. A cisgender woman, for example, has female reproductive parts and identifies as a woman.
- **Gay** refers to any person who is attracted to someone of the same gender.
- **Heterosexual** refers to someone who is exclusively attracted to people of the opposite gender. For instance, a man who is attracted only to women.
- **Intersex** refers to someone who is born with both male and female or ambiguous reproductive and/or sexual anatomy.
- **Lesbian** is a term for women who are attracted to women. Some women who are attracted to women prefer the terms gay or queer instead.
- **Nonbinary** refers to someone who rejects or does not identify with the gender binary of man or woman. A person may identify as both man and woman simultaneously, in fluctuation, as something else entirely, or as no gender at all.
- **Pansexual** refers to people whose attraction to folks does not depend on gender identity.
- **Queer** is an umbrella term that can be used to describe people within the LGBTQIAP+ community or can be used by people who reject any specific identity. It is important to note that queer is a reclaimed term, a term that was previously used in a disparaging way, and thus, some LGBTQIAP+ people may embrace this term, while others reject it.
- **Questioning** refers to someone who is currently questioning their sexual identity, gender identity, gender expression, or some combination of the three and might be in the process of exploration.
- **Two-Spirit** refers to Indigenous peoples who identify as having both masculine and feminine spirits. Two-Spirit is considered a separate, third gender in some Indigenous communities, although the term used to describe a Two-Spirit individual may vary within certain groups. For example, the Navajo tribe uses the term Nádleehí for Two-Spirit individuals, and the Zuni tribe uses the term Lhamana.

NOT INCLUSIVE	MORE INCLUSIVE	HERE'S WHY
He or She Ladies and Gentlemen	Ask for pronouns They, them, theirs Everyone	These noninclusive terms imply that gender is binary (either man or woman) and don't acknowledge the broad spectrum of gender identity. Inclusive language ensures that all people are acknowledged.
Homosexual	Gay, Lesbian, Bisexual, Pansexual, Queer, etc. (Important: Ask individuals which term they use for themselves.)	The word *homosexual* was historically tied to the now-discredited notion of a psychological disorder and is therefore considered offensive. Avoid using it. Note that the term *queer* may be offensive to those who have experienced its use as a slur. However, the term has also been reclaimed as a self-identifier. This example helps show why it is important to listen for or ask people which terms they identify with.
Male/Female	Man/Woman	*Male* and *female* refer to biological sex. When it is pertinent to a conversation or written communication, refer to an individual's gender identity instead, and when it's not, use a genderless term like those listed below.
Man the booth Mankind Man-made You guys Policeman Fireman Freshman	Staff the booth Humankind Human-made, human-caused, artificial, synthetic Friends, colleagues, everyone, all, team, everybody Police officer Firefighter First-year student	Using man as a generic term excludes women and nonbinary individuals. Inclusive language acknowledges that people of all identities are included and may serve in any capacity.
Mr./Mrs./Ms.	First or last name Mx. Dr., Reverend, Rabbi	Using titles can be problematic if you're not certain of a person's gender identity, marital status, or professional title. Mr./Mrs./Ms. also exclude those outside of the man/woman binary. When possible, refer to people by their first or last name instead. Mx. is another gender-neutral option. Use professional titles for those who hold those designations.

NOT INCLUSIVE	MORE INCLUSIVE	HERE'S WHY
What are your preferred pronouns?	What are your pronouns?	A person's pronouns are consistent with their gender identity. Using the term *preferred pronouns* implies that these words are their choice versus inherent to who they are.
Straight	Heterosexual	Avoid the term *straight*. It implies that nonheterosexual people are somehow in the wrong or not normal.
Transgendered	Transgender	The word *transgender* is an adjective, not a verb or a noun. Putting the extraneous "-ed" at the end is grammatically incorrect. Likewise, it is incorrect to say, "Tony is a transgender," or "The parade included many transgenders." Instead, say "Tony is a transgender person," or "Many transgender people marched in the parade."

HANDBOOK EXERCISES

THERE'S A WORD FOR THAT

Correctly fill in the blanks in the following sentences using one of these terms:

(a) agender (b) asexual (c) pronouns (d) gender (e) misgender (f) cisgender (g) bigender (h) bisexual (i) sex

1. Marco had long blond hair as a child. Adults would often _____ him as a girl. As an adult, he has always identified as a _____ man, consistent with the sex he was assigned at birth. Over the years he has had romantic relationships with both women and men and personally identifies as _____.

2. Tory was assigned the _____ of girl at birth and has always used the _____ she, her, and hers. At the same time, she feels neutral about her gender and therefore identifies as _____.

THE CONTEXT QUIZ

Make your best guess!

1. What percentage of adults in the United States identify as LGBTQ+? _____

2. What percentage of millennials (those aged 24 to 39 in 2020) who identify as LGBTQ+ say they are bisexual? _____

3. Is the word transgender a(n) (a) verb, (b) adjective, or (c) noun?

IMAGINE THIS

You have a new client. So far, you have only communicated via email and text. Just before your first face-to-face meeting, you realize that you're unsure of your client's gender. Sometimes, you perceive them as a woman; at other times as a man. Your client's first name is not helping you to decide, and you can't find their pronouns listed online. How would you proceed with learning from your client the way they wish to be addressed in conversation and in writing? How would you share this information with your colleagues who are also on the client team?

_____

_____

_____

UPON REFLECTION

Think about this: If you identify as LGBTQ+, what has made you feel the most welcomed/included at your current company? And what has made you feel the most unwelcome/excluded? If you do not identify as LGBTQ+, how could you go about learning what your LGBTQ+ colleagues think about your company's LGBTQ+ inclusion? Write down your thoughts in brief bullet points.

_____

_____

_____

RECOMMENDED READING/VIEWING/LISTENING
- Watch *Stonewall Uprising, Paris Is Burning, The Death and Life of Marsha P. Johnson*, and other LGBTQ+ documentaries.
- There are many podcasts that inform, entertain, and build community among LGBTQ+ people and allies. Three to start with are *LGBTQ&A, One From the Vaults*, and *Nancy*.

- Visit the It Gets Better Project website and watch one or more short videos. Listen to stories of people who identify with genders or sexual orientations that you're unfamiliar with.

THERE'S A WORD FOR THAT—ANSWERS

(e) misgender; (f) cisgender; (h) bisexual;

(d) gender; (c) pronouns; (a) agender

THE CONTEXT QUIZ—ANSWERS

1. 7.1% of adults in the United States identify as LGBTQ+ according to a 2021 Gallup poll.[27]
2. 54% of millennials (those aged 24 to 39 in 2020) who identify as LGBTQ+ say they are bisexual.[28]
3. (b) The word transgender is an adjective.

2 DISABILITY AND INVISIBLE ILLNESS

Did you know that 26% of adults in the United States have some type of disability and that 60% of adults in the United States have a chronic disease?[29] Discriminatory and derogatory terms for people with disabilities typically generalize the entire population and diminish the value of individual personhood. To speak inclusively instead, remember our number one guideline: put people first. When we describe someone as handicapped, for example, we reduce the complexity and fullness of their humanity. We define them only by their diagnosis, disability, or condition.

Just because a person has a disability does not mean they are disabled. By using person-first language, we acknowledge that the person may live with that part of their identity, but they are not defined by it. At the same time, it's important to note that, within the disability community, there are varying views on the difference between the terms "disabled person" versus "person with a disability." We encourage you to read more on this topic.[30]

Also, reject purposely softened expressions like "differently abled." While intended to be inoffensive, they instead suggest that there is something shameful about having a disability. Terms like "suffers from," "hero," "saint," and "soldier" should also be avoided. They exaggerate emotion and imply a one-dimensional character versus a multidimensional person.

Here, it's important to recognize and understand invisible disabilities and invisible illnesses as well. These terms refer to a wide range of medical conditions and diagnoses that impact a person's life, but are not immediately apparent to others. Many of these disabilities are neurological in nature; some are chronic or incurable. The list includes sleep disorders, joint problems, diabetes, phobias, chronic pain, autoimmune diseases, and fibromyalgia. An estimated 10% of people in the United States have an invisible illness that may not be apparent in their day-to-day professional interactions.[31] In the absence of visible evidence, these conditions are often belittled, ignored, or trivialized.

As a general rule, listen to the words that people use to talk about themselves, and try to mirror their language. Review this table to learn more:

NOT INCLUSIVE	MORE INCLUSIVE	HERE'S WHY
Birth defect	Person with a congenital disability Person with a birth anomaly	The word *defect* implies a person is broken or somehow incomplete.
The Blind The Deaf	Person who is blind or vision impaired Person who is Deaf or hard of hearing	These noninclusive terms align identity only with the person's condition or impairment. Put the person first. Also note that *Deaf* should always be capitalized.
CP victim Spastic Spaz	Person with cerebral palsy Person with spastic cerebral palsy	Using these terms is offensive. Noninclusive terms imply that people with cerebral palsy are not normal.
Dumb Mute Deaf-mute	Person who cannot speak, has difficulty speaking, uses synthetic speech, is nonvocal, or is nonverbal	The terms *dumb* and *mute* were once widely used to describe people who could not speak; *deaf-mute* was used to refer to people who could neither speak nor hear. These imply that people are incapable of expressing themselves. However, people living with speech and hearing disabilities are capable of expressing themselves in many ways.
Epileptic	Person with epilepsy Person with a seizure disorder	Acknowledge that the individual lives with a condition but is not defined by it.

NOT INCLUSIVE	MORE INCLUSIVE	HERE'S WHY
Handicapped Disabled Crippled Suffers from Afflicted with Victim of Invalid Lame Deformed	Person with a disability People with disabilities A person who uses leg braces, a person in a wheelchair, a person with Autism, etc.	These noninclusive terms imply that people with disabilities are not capable. Instead, acknowledge the disability, but do not use it to define someone. The terms *handicap* and *handicapped* have fallen out of favor in all uses relating to physical and mental disabilities. While not as offensive as some terms, it is also not preferable to use the words *disabled* or *impaired*.
Handicapped parking	Accessible parking Parking for people with disabilities	These inclusive terms help you replace the noninclusive term *handicapped*.
Normal person	It is never appropriate to use this phrase to describe a person.	The term *normal* implies that other people are abnormal.
Paraplegic/ Quadriplegic	Person with a spinal cord injury Person with paraplegia Person who is paralyzed	Like so many other terms for physical conditions, these noninclusive terms generalize the population and minimize personhood. Acknowledge the person first.
Wheelchair bound Confined or restricted to a wheelchair	Person who uses a wheelchair Wheelchair user	The inclusive terms acknowledge that the person may use a wheelchair as a tool but is not confined, bound, or restricted to it.
Lame	Boring, unexciting, uncool	You can easily describe something that is not engaging in a number of ways that don't make a negative reference to disability.

HANDBOOK EXERCISES

THERE'S A WORD FOR THAT

Correctly fill in the blanks in the following sentences using one of these terms:

(a) Deaf (b) autoimmune (c) visually impaired (d) accessible (e) blind (f) hard of hearing (g) handicapped

    1. Ruth is in charge of updating the technology in her company's auditorium. She realizes that an onstage presentation screen might be helpful to people who are _____ or _____ but not people who are _____ or _____.

    2. Tomas is updating his company's building and grounds signage. To ensure the language is inclusive and not offensive, he's changing all references of _____ to _____ instead, including the signs in the parking lots.

THE CONTEXT QUIZ

Make your best guess!

What percentage of adults in the United States:

    1. Have some type of disability? _____

    2. Have an invisible illness? _____

What percentage of people with a disability:

    3. Have a mobility disability with serious difficulty walking or climbing stairs? _____

    4. Have a cognition disability with serious difficulty concentrating, remembering, or making decisions? _____

    5. Are Deaf or have serious difficulty hearing? _____

    6. Have a vision disability with blindness or serious difficulty seeing even when wearing glasses? _____

IMAGINE THIS

You are in charge of planning a team-building retreat for your work group. You want to make sure that the location, activities, meals, and schedule are inclusive and comfortable for everyone. What steps would you take to accomplish this? How would you involve your teammates in the planning process?

_____

_____

_____

UPON REFLECTION

What initiatives have you seen your company take to accommodate the needs of employees with disabilities? Have you noticed steps they haven't taken, yet that would help ensure all employees can do their best work? Write down your thoughts in brief bullet points.

_____

_____

_____

RECOMMENDED READING/VIEWING/LISTENING

- *Forbes* publishes a short list of eight great podcasts about disability.[32] Among them are *Barrier Free Futures* and *Power Not Pity*.
- The Invisible Disabilities Association raises awareness of invisible disabilities in the six-minute video "Bringing Visibility to Invisible Disabilities and Invisible Illness," available on YouTube.[33]
- The *Make It Work* employment empowerment video series[34] from the World Institute on Disability addresses workplace issues for people with disabilities.

THERE'S A WORD FOR THAT—ANSWERS

1. (b) Deaf; (f) hearing impaired; (e) blind; (c) visually impaired
2. (g) handicapped; (d) accessible

THE CONTEXT QUIZ—ANSWERS [Source: CDC]

1. 26% of adults in the United States have some type of disability.
2. 10% of people in the United States have an invisible illness.
3. 13.7% of people with a disability have a mobility disability with serious difficulty walking or climbing stairs.
4. 10.8% of people with a disability have a cognition disability with serious difficulty concentrating, remembering, or making decisions.
5. 5.9% of people with a disability are Deaf or have serious difficulty hearing.
6. 4.6% of people with a disability have a vision disability with blindness or serious difficulty seeing even when wearing glasses.

3 MENTAL, EMOTIONAL, AND COGNITIVE DIVERSITY

Many people casually interchange words that describe mental and emotional health diagnoses with words that describe everyday moods and behaviors. Doing this can trivialize the impact of actual medical conditions. For example, saying that someone who is sad is "depressed" or that someone who pays incredible attention to detail is "OCD" is inaccurate and an exaggeration.

Some people also use terms like retarded, idiot, demented, and so on. These derogatory expressions are holdovers from an era when mental and emotional health treatment was often unenlightened, discriminatory, and abusive. Practicing inclusive language requires staying alert to these detrimental words, phrases, and attitudes, and replacing them with accurate, respectful terms.

Defining a person's complete identity by their cognitive processing (such as "he is ADHD") is based on the false construct that some people think "normally" while others do not. It excludes people with diverse ways of thinking, or *neurodiversity*. This term has only recently gained widespread acknowledgement. In brief, neurodiversity refers to the natural variations in human brain functions, especially around learning, thinking, and processing information.

Still, the term is often applied too narrowly, only to people with autism spectrum disorder, attention deficit hyperactivity disorder, or dyslexia. It's important to consider this concept more broadly by recognizing that neurodiversity is not a deficit, abnormality, or problem to be solved. Rather, it is a difference that individuals and teams can leverage for greater results. For example, research shows that people with ADHD are often highly creative, innovative, and entrepreneurial. Many people with autism show greater-than-average attention to detail and display strong focus skills.

Note also that some people may not have a medical diagnosis but have certain beneficial ways of thinking and organizing their work. For example, some people are excellent at remembering names, others at remembering numbers. Some have excellent drawing and visualization skills. Embracing neurodiversity means recognizing the broad range of natural human cognitive functioning and respecting our differences as strengths within teams and organizations.

Additionally, describing a person's level of intelligence in negative terms is insulting. Yes, some people have diagnosed disabilities that impact them intellectually, physically, or both. While it's acceptable to use these terms when accurate and relevant, it's preferable to use the name of the specific disability whenever possible and remember to only mention it if it's relevant to the conversation.

Inclusive language avoids derogatory and insulting words and expressions when talking about mental, emotional, and cognitive diversity. It encourages us to embrace the differences each person offers. It requires that we speak more literally and specifically to remove mental and emotional health stigmas. Review this table to learn more:

LESS INCLUSIVE	MORE INCLUSIVE	HERE'S WHY
ADHD	Neurodivergent A person with ADHD	Saying a person "is ADHD" makes this medical condition the single defining trait of their identity and minimizes their personhood.
Anorexic/Bulimic	A person with an eating disorder	*Anorexia* and *bulimia* are psychological disorders. These terms should only be used in a valid medical context. Referring to a person as anorexic/bulimic to describe their physicality is a negative judgment that minimizes their personhood. Never assume why a person's body looks the way it does.
Autistic	Neurodivergent A person with autism spectrum disorder	Saying a person is *autistic* generalizes the population and minimizes personhood. Use this term only when medically valid, self-identified, and relevant to the conversation. Autism is a developmental disorder, not an intellectual disability. In fact, most people with autism display average or above-average intelligence.
Crazy Nuts Maniac Lunatic Insane Deranged Psycho Demented	Surprising, wild, shocking, absurd, exciting, unreal, amazing, wonderful, remarkable, extraordinary	Using derogatory terms to describe behavior that is surprising or unexpected minimizes and stigmatizes the impacts of real mental health conditions.
Depressed OCD PTSD	Sad Organized, particular Traumatized, fearful, has bad memories	Don't use the terms *depression, OCD, PTSD,* or any other mental health diagnosis to casually describe someone's occasional moods or behaviors.

LESS INCLUSIVE	MORE INCLUSIVE	HERE'S WHY
Slow learner Stupid	Person with a learning disability	A *learning disability* is any mental condition that prevents a person from acquiring the same amount of knowledge as others in their age group. A learning disability is not an intellectual disability. In fact, individuals with learning disabilities typically display average or above-average intelligence.
Retarded Moron Idiot Imbecile	Person with an intellectual or cognitive disability Developmental disability IDD	*Intellectual disability* starts any time before a child reaches age 18 and is characterized by differences with both: • Intellectual functioning or intelligence, which include the ability to learn, reason, problem solve, and other skills. • Adaptive behavior, which includes everyday social and life skills. The term *developmental disabilities* is a broader category of often lifelong challenges that can be intellectual, physical, or both. *IDD* is the term often used to describe the combination of intellectual disability and other disabilities.
Down's person	Person with Down syndrome	*Down syndrome* is a genetic disorder that causes intellectual disability. You should only refer to this condition when the diagnosis has been shared and it is relevant to the conversation. Also, note that the respectful term does not include the apostrophe and final "s."
Special needs	A person with . . .	Although once the accepted term in educational settings for students who required assistance for disabilities, this phrase is disrespectful and offensive when used as a noun or as a casual joke. Instead, use literal and specific language that begins: *a person with* . . .

LESS INCLUSIVE	MORE INCLUSIVE	HERE'S WHY
Senile Dementia/ Demented	Person with Alzheimer's disease Person who has dementia	*Dementia* is not a specific illness but a general term used to describe a decline in mental ability that interferes with daily life. *Alzheimer's disease* is the most common form of dementia. Only use these terms when medically accurate and relevant.

HANDBOOK EXERCISES

THERE'S A WORD FOR THAT

Correctly fill in the blanks in the following sentences using one of these terms:

(a) learning disability (b) developmental disabilities (c) autism spectrum disorder (d) dyslexia (e) cognitive disability (f) neurodiversity

1. David's agency hires people with _____ such as ADHD, Down syndrome, and expressive language disorder.

2. Katya's daughter was having trouble reading and was reversing the order of letters. She was diagnosed with a common type of _____ called_____.

3. Angela was amazed at how increasing the _____of her team increased their ability to solve problems more quickly and creatively.

THE CONTEXT QUIZ

Make your best guess!

1. What percentage of adults in the United States have a learning disability? _____

2. True or False: The terms intellectual disability, cognitive disability, and learning disability all have the same meaning. _____

3. What percentage of US adults with intellectual disability (ID) are employed? _____

IMAGINE THIS

You have just hired a new salesperson who has dyslexia. They're doing a fantastic job with in-person presentations, but their written sales reports are disorganized, poorly written, and filled with spelling errors. How would you go about discussing the situation with this employee? What ways might you explore to further leverage their strengths and provide them with alternate ways of reporting?

_____

_____

_____

UPON REFLECTION

Think of a time when your work team brainstormed to solve a challenging problem. How did having diverse viewpoints and ways of thinking contribute to finding a better solution? Write down your thoughts in brief bullet points.

_____

_____

_____

RECOMMENDED READING/VIEWING/LISTENING

- Research the official style guide from the National Center on Disability and Journalism, which recommends dozens of words and terms to use when referring to disability.[35]
- The National Institute of Health (NIH) provides an in-depth description of Intellectual and Developmental Disabilities.[36]
- The Neurodiversity Network suggests a number of podcasts related to neurodiversity, autism, employment, empowerment, and quality of life. Two to start with are *Neuroverse by Groktopus* and *All in the Mind.*[37]

THERE'S A WORD FOR THAT—ANSWERS

1. (b) developmental disabilities
2. (a) learning disability; (d) dyslexia
3. (f) neurodiversity

THE CONTEXT QUIZ—ANSWERS

1. According to the National Institutes of Health, 15% of the US population, or 1 in 7 Americans, has some type of learning disability.[38] Difficulty with basic reading and language skills are the most common learning disabilities.

2. False. Intellectual disability and cognitive disability share the same meaning—when a person has certain limitations in mental functioning and in skills such as communication, self-help, and social skills. Learning disabilities are not the same thing; difficulty with basic reading and language skills are the most common learning disabilities.

3. Only 44% of adults with intellectual disability (ID) are in the workforce. And 28% of working age adults with ID have never held a job.[39]

4 PHYSICALITY

Practicing inclusive language around physical differences acknowledges the wide range of natural human diversity. It makes every person in the room feel welcome and respected, no matter their size, shape, skin, hair, or any other physical factor.

It bears repeating: there's no such thing as normal. To activate the benefits of a diverse team and welcome every voice at the table, it's important to avoid terms and phrases that create or reinforce stigmas, shame, or stereotypes about people's bodies. Some of these terms inappropriately use real medical conditions to describe common and natural physical diversity. Other terms show an unconscious bias toward a certain body size or shape.

It's best practice not to mention a person's physical appearance at all. Usually, doing so is inappropriate, unnecessary, and irrelevant. Instead, look for more professional and appropriate identity descriptors. "He is the person who works at the corner desk." "They are the person in the yellow, button-down blouse." "She is the person second from the right." Take time to consider which descriptors are relevant or irrelevant to your conversation. Review this table to learn more:

LESS INCLUSIVE	MORE INCLUSIVE	HERE'S WHY
Dwarf Midget	A person with dwarfism Little person	Dwarfism is a medical or genetic condition that results in a stature less than 4 feet 10 inches, according to the Little People of America organization. This term should only be used in a medical context. The term *midget*, used in the past to describe an unusually short person, is now widely considered to be derogatory.

LESS INCLUSIVE	MORE INCLUSIVE	HERE'S WHY
Fat Overweight Obese Heavy Big	Avoid these terms entirely	It is never appropriate to use physical descriptors of size or shape. Instead, use professional, inoffensive, and relevant descriptors to identify an individual, such as, "Their sales manager is sitting to the right of the CEO," or "She was the woman in the blue suit."
Skinny Anorexic Skin and bones	Avoid these terms entirely	Again, it is never appropriate to use physical descriptors of size or shape. Use professional, relevant descriptors instead.

HANDBOOK EXERCISES

THE CONTEXT QUIZ

Make your best guess!

1. In a 2017 survey, 500 hiring professionals were shown photos of potential job candidates. What percentage said they would consider hiring an individual who appeared very overweight? _____
2. True or False: Taller people tend to earn more money during their careers. _____
3. What percentage of little people are born to parents of average height? _____

IMAGINE THIS

Your boss is deciding who will represent your company at an upcoming trade show. She has selected you, but you notice that she did not select two of the most experienced and knowledgeable salespeople on your team. You're not sure if this was a factor in his selection, but one of these individuals is a little person and the other is a person who uses a wheelchair. You feel that their experience and expertise is needed at the booth. How would you approach your boss to discuss this?

_____

_____

_____

UPON REFLECTION

Have you ever noticed a hiring or other business decision at your company that seemed to be influenced by the physicality of the individual? If so, how did this occurrence make you feel about equity and inclusion at your company? What steps do you think management could take to eliminate choices based on physicality and ensure equal opportunities for all employees? Write down your thoughts in brief bullet points.

_____

_____

_____

RECOMMENDED READING/VIEWING/LISTENING

- Read the article "100 Words to Describe Coworkers (and Why You Should Use Them)" from Indeed.[40]
- Commenting on physicality is a form of workplace incivility. Read "The Price of Incivility" from *Harvard Business Review* for an in-depth explanation.[41]
- *Real Simple* recommends 10 body-positive podcasts related to the anti-diet movement, body acceptance, health, and well-being. Among them are "Eat the Rules" and "Yes and Body Politics."[42]

THE CONTEXT QUIZ—ANSWERS

1. According to CNBC, only 15.6% of the hiring professionals surveyed said they would consider hiring the candidate who appeared the most overweight.[43]
2. True. Multiple studies have shown that for each additional inch of height, people earn an average of roughly $800 more annually. For example, someone who is 6 feet tall earns an average of about $5,525 more than someone who is 7 inches shorter.[44]
3. Approximately 80% of little people are born to parents of average height.[45]

5 CULTURAL DIVERSITY: RACE, ETHNICITY, AND NATIONALITY

As a first step to understanding the context and terminology of cultural diversity, it's helpful to recognize the difference between race and ethnicity. "Race is understood by most people as a mixture of physical, behavioral, and cultural attributes. Ethnicity recognizes differences between people mostly on the basis of language and shared culture," according to Nina Jablonski, an anthropologist and paleobiologist at Pennsylvania State University.[46]

It is estimated that, as a species, humans share 99.9% of our DNA with one other.[47] Our physical differences are determined by only a minute portion of the human genome. The few differences that *do* exist between people reflect variations in environments and external factors, not core biology.

Modern scientists prefer the term "ancestry" rather than "race." Race is a cultural construct, not a biological attribute. Therefore, biologically speaking, race does not exist. Ancestry speaks to a person's genetic history, while race relies only on social categorization. Still, race is an important part of many people's individual identity, and so, we should strive to use the most respectful terms and words for racial groups.

When choosing inclusive terms to describe someone's cultural identity, never assume that you know a person's racial, ethnic, or national descriptors based on their appearance. Also avoid making assumptions based on a person's name, language, accent, or dialect. Keep in mind that a person's race and ethnicity may not match their nationality and every person will have multiple, intersectional identities. Your second-generation Latina accountant, for example, may identify simultaneously as Latine, Argentine, Hispanic, and American.[48]

Consider whether learning the particulars of a person's cultural identity is relevant to your conversation at that moment. If it is, avoid offensive questions such as "What are you?" or "Where are you from?" Instead, say "May I ask your ethnicity?" Review this table to learn more:

NOT INCLUSIVE	MORE INCLUSIVE	HERE'S WHY
American	US citizen Person from the United States	The area of the Americas includes 35 separate countries. Yet, when people in the United States talk about Americans, they're often referring to people only from the United States. Doing so fails to acknowledge the other countries within this geography. Specifically reference the United States instead.
Colored	Person of color	Avoid using the highly offensive racial slur *colored*. This term was often used during segregation to separate people of color, particularly Black people, from "Whites Only" restaurants, bathrooms, drinking fountains, and seats on public transportation. Designated "colored" spaces were the least-desirable and most poorly maintained locations and spaces. By contrast, the term *person of color* is not offensive. It can be used to describe any culturally diverse person.

NOT INCLUSIVE	MORE INCLUSIVE	HERE'S WHY
	Black African American	*Black* is a term that encompasses people whose ancestors descend from the African diaspora. In the United States, some people identify as Black, and others identify as African American. If this distinction is relevant to your conversation, ask the person which term they use for themselves.
	African Afro-Caribbean	The term *African American* is understood to mean a person from the United States. People from Africa are Africans. People of color who are from the Caribbean region may use the term *Afro-Caribbean*. Calling people from Africa and the Caribbean "African Americans" is therefore incorrect. Be specific about referencing a person's particular country of origin whenever possible.
Eskimo	Indigenous Refer to a person's specific tribe	The term *Eskimo* has historically been used to stereotype and demean Indigenous and Inuit people. Use the term *Indigenous* instead. Whenever possible, refer to a person's specific tribe. Also, learn more about the differences between the terms *Indigenous, native, first peoples, Aboriginal*, and more.
Hispanic Latinx	Latina, Latino Latine Reference the person's country of origin (e.g., Cuban)	The term *Hispanic* is widely used to describe individuals from Spanish-speaking countries. However, you should avoid referring to someone as Hispanic based on their name or appearance. Check with them first to learn how they identify. Many people with Central and South American Indigenous ancestry (e.g., Mayan, Mexican) reject the term Hispanic because it incorrectly implies their ancestors came from Spain. The term *Latinx*, which was introduced in recent years with the intention of being inclusive, has proven to feel exclusionary to most people. Recent national surveys of people from Latin America show that the term Latinx is highly unpopular. Influential media and advocacy groups have started dropping the term or even arguing against its use. As a genderless term, you may choose *Latine* (pronounced "Latin-ay") instead.[48]

NOT INCLUSIVE	MORE INCLUSIVE	HERE'S WHY
Illegal immigrant Alien	Born in [country] Immigrant Undocumented immigrant Refugee (for asylum seekers)	Describing a person as *illegal* dehumanizes them. It implies that they are a criminal and brands them as personally illegitimate. By contrast, the term *undocumented immigrant* avoids these negative connotations. It references a person's actions, not their personhood. Use the term *refugees* for people who have been forced to leave their country to escape war, persecution, or natural disaster.
Indian	Native American Indigenous Refer to a person's specific tribe	In the United States, using the term *Indian* to describe Indigenous people took root when Christopher Columbus mistook the Caribbean islands for those in the Indian Ocean. Although this term is still commonly heard today, it is also often associated with the subjugation and decimation of Indigenous people and cultures that began when Europeans arrived in the Americas and continued after the formation of the United States. Note that, in writing, it is correct to capitalize the word "Indigenous" when referring to a specific group or person, just as you would capitalize other ethnic and cultural identities, like Black or Jewish.
Oriental	Asian Person of Asian descent Asian American Refer to a person's identified race or ethnicity	People from Asia are Asian. Only use the term *Oriental* to describe objects, such as artwork or rugs. Some people of Asian ancestry in the United States identify with the term Asian American while others do not. Asia comprises 48 separate countries, according to the United Nations. Be specific about referencing a person's particular country of origin whenever possible. If this topic is relevant to your conversation, ask the person how they identify. As a universal best practice, you may say "a person of Asian ancestry" or "people of Asian descent."
Slave	Enslaved people	The term *slave* dehumanizes individuals. The condition of slavery does not define who individuals are as people.

HANDBOOK EXERCISES

THERE'S A WORD FOR THAT

Correctly fill in the blanks in the following sentences using one of these terms:

(a) intersectionality (b) nationality (c) African (d) race (e) Filipino (f) Indigenous (g) African American (h) ethnic

1. Vladimir was born in the United States. His mother's ancestors are from the Mapuche group, which is native to Chile, so his mom's side of the family is composed of _____ people. His father was born in Madrid, so his dad's first _____ was Spanish. Vladimir is proud of all aspects of his _____ identity.

2. Vanessa was born in Zimbabwe. In the United States, many people mistakenly refer to her as _____, when actually she is _____. She is also of mixed _____and finds it usually takes time for people to understand and appreciate the _____ of her identity.

THE CONTEXT QUIZ

Make your best guess!

1. What percentage of the US population is Indigenous? _____
2. What percentage of US workers were born in another country? _____
3. If you were born outside of the United States, what is the process of becoming a US citizen called?

IMAGINE THIS

Your company is headquartered in a culturally diverse city and has a diverse workforce and customer base. You have been asked to lead the design and implementation of a multi-cultural day of celebration. Who would you invite to join your planning committee? How would you make your event and your promotional materials inclusive?

_____

_____

_____

UPON REFLECTION

If you were born outside of the United States, what has made you feel the most welcomed or included at your current company? And, what has made you feel the most unwelcome or excluded?

_____

_____

_____

If you were born in the United States, how could you go about learning what your colleagues born in other countries think about your company's state of inclusion? Write down your thoughts in brief bullet points.

_____

_____

_____

RECOMMENDED READING/VIEWING/LISTENING

- Ongig has compiled a Top 10 list of videos regarding cultural diversity developed by US corporations. Check out Caterpillar Inc.'s "Inclusion at Work," Expedia Group's "Everybody Always Everywhere," and _Purl_ by Pixar SparkShorts.[49]
- The _Latino USA_ podcast offers insight into the lived experiences of Latine communities and cultural, political, and social ideas impacting Latine people and the nation.[50]
- There are many podcasts to better understand the Black experience, including _Code Switch_, _Still Processing_, and _Pod Save the People_.
- Podcasts that explore the complexity and richness of Asian American and Pacific Islander identity include _Self Evident: Asian America's Stories_, _Southern Fried Asian_, and _This Filipino American Life_.[51]

THERE'S A WORD FOR THAT—ANSWERS

1. (f) Indigenous; (b) nationality; (h) ethnic
2. (g) African American; (c) African; (d) race; (a) intersectionality

THE CONTEXT QUIZ—ANSWERS

1. Around 6.6 million people in the United States, or 2% of the total population, identify as Native American or Alaskan Native, either alone or in combination with another ethnic identity.[52]

2. There were 28.4 million foreign-born workers in the United States in 2019, who made up 17.4% of the total workforce.[53]

3. Naturalization is the process to become a US citizen if you were born outside of the United States.

6 RELIGION

Every country in the world contains a multitude of religious identities and expressions. People sometimes make assumptions about a person's religion based on that person's race or ethnicity, and these assumptions are often inaccurate. For example, not all Arab people are Muslim, and not all Buddhist people have Asian ancestry. A sizable percentage of people practice no religion at all; about 3 in 10 US adults are religiously unaffiliated, according to the Pew Research Forum.[54]

Many individuals are comfortable describing their own faith by saying, for example, "I'm a Catholic" or "I'm a Jew." This structure uses the proper noun form of the religion. However, if you're describing another person's religious identity, we recommend that you use an adjective instead. For example, say "Van follows Buddhist traditions" or "Anna is a member of the Baptist faith." This grammatical practice is a good way to acknowledge that the person you're referencing has an intersectional identity and is not defined as an individual by their religion alone.

Some people may identify culturally with the religion of their family or their ancestors, but not identify as religiously observant themselves. They may not feel comfortable with any religious descriptor at all. A person who celebrates Easter and Christmas, for example, may not identify as Christian. A person of Hindu ancestry who does not practice Hinduism may not personally identify as Hindu.

As with so many other realms of diversity, never assume that you know a person's religious identity or ancestry based on their appearance, ethnicity, culture, or nationality. Review this table for more recommendations:

LESS INCLUSIVE	MORE INCLUSIVE	HERE'S WHY
Jew The Jews	Member of the Jewish faith Follower of Judaism Jewish person	For millennia, at different times and places worldwide, people of the Jewish faith have periodically been subject to discrimination and hatred. This anti-Semitism persists today. It's typical for people who are Jewish to self-identify by saying "I'm Jewish" or "I'm a Jew." For those who are not Jewish, best practice is to use Jewish as an adjective and not as a noun. For instance, you may say you have Jewish friends or refer to the history of the Jewish people.

LESS INCLUSIVE	MORE INCLUSIVE	HERE'S WHY
Islamic	Muslim person/people Person of the Islamic faith	Use the adjective *Islamic* to describe art, texts, architecture, etc., that relate to the religion of Islam. *Muslim* is also an adjective of or relating to the religion, law, or civilization of Islam. It is also the appropriate word for people who practice the Islamic faith. Always say "Muslim" when you are referring to people.
Mormon LDS	A member of The Church of Jesus Christ of Latter-day Saints Latter-day saint	In their official style guide, The Church of Jesus Christ of Latter-day Saints requests that the full name of their religion be used.[55] When a shortened reference is needed, they indicate that the terms "the Church," the "Church of Jesus Christ," and the "restored Church of Jesus Christ" are also accurate and encouraged. *Latter-day saints* is the appropriate way to describe individuals of this faith.

HANDBOOK EXERCISES

THERE'S A WORD FOR THAT

Correctly fill in the blanks in the following sentences using one of these terms:

(a) imam (b) unaffiliated (c) Islam (d) rabbi (e) mosque (f) Buddhism (g) synagogue (h) interfaith

1. Frank told his coworkers that he and his fiancé were planning to get married at their church, with the minister officiating. His Muslim colleague shared that she and her husband were married at their _____, where the service was led by their _____. His Jewish colleague said that he belonged to a _____, but that he and his partner were going to have a commitment ceremony at a botanical garden, with their _____ officiating.

2. After the devastating hurricane, multiple religious congregations gathered for a(n) _____ service. Many local residents who are _____ religiously also attended.

THE CONTEXT QUIZ

Make your best guess!

1. What percentage of people in the world identify as Christian, Muslim, and Jewish respectively? _____; _____; _____

2. Are US employers required to allow employees to have religious holidays off? _____

3. Diwali is one of the most important holidays of what religion? _____

IMAGINE THIS

You're having a casual conversation with several coworkers in the coffee break room. One of them makes a derogatory remark in reference to people of a particular religion, acting as if it's a joke. What do you say to them?

_____

_____

_____

UPON REFLECTION

What's the difference between civic and religious holidays in terms of how they are noted in the workplace? What should be the difference between how the company marks holidays versus how individual employees do? What policies do you think would make the workplace environment inclusive and comfortable for all, regardless of their religion?

_____

_____

_____

RECOMMENDED READING/VIEWING/LISTENING

- The short video, "Employment Law: Religious Discrimination in the Workplace," from LawShelf explains how employment law applies to religious discrimination in the workplace.[56]
- In "The Real Meaning of the Separation of Church and State," *Time* magazine defines and provides the history of the separation of church and state in the United States.[57]
- Read the actionable article "3 Ways to Build a Religiously Inclusive Work Culture," by Raafi-Karim Alidina and Human Resource Executive.[58]

THERE'S A WORD FOR THAT—ANSWERS

1. (e) mosque; (a) imam; (g) synagogue; (d) rabbi

2. (h) interfaith; (b) unaffiliated

THE CONTEXT QUIZ—ANSWERS

1. As of 2020, approximately 31% worldwide identify as Christian; 25% as Muslim; and 0.18% as Jewish.[59]

2. Employers with 15 or more employees must make reasonable accommodations for employees' religious observances, according to Title VII of the Civil Rights Act of 1964.

3. Diwali is one of the major festivals in the Hindu religion.

7 ACQUIRED DIVERSITY

So far, we have talked almost exclusively about inclusive language for inherent diversity: the traits a person has at birth. Acquired diversity, by contrast, refers to characteristics and ways of thinking that a person gains through life experience. Acquired diversity includes a broad range of factors such as age, education, marital status, family structure, immigration status, travel, trauma, veteran status, and conflict.

To practice inclusive language for acquired diversity, avoid idioms and slang terms that reference real traumas like addiction, poverty, incarceration, or challenging life events like divorce. Idioms and slang trivialize the impact of people's difficult experiences. They reinforce community stigmas and convey bias toward people who have suffered trauma. They also work as microaggressions, silencing people who have had those experiences.

For example, stay away from exaggerations like "I'm starving today" or "She's addicted to coffee." Such statements ignore the reality that some people experience real hunger and real addiction. If you say "this negotiation is a war," it evokes the image of a life-threatening crisis where none exists. Say "this has been a difficult negotiation" instead.

In the same way that workforce teams with inherent diversity deliver better problem-solving and creative innovation for a business, acquired diversity brings a vast range of experiences and perspectives to the table. A broad spectrum of people who express different viewpoints and have built their lives from varied experiences will inevitably lead to more-creative problem-solving and a richer, more interesting workplace culture.

Practicing inclusive language helps to create an equitable and accessible environment for all people, regardless of their past or present experiences. Review this table for more examples:

LESS INCLUSIVE	MORE INCLUSIVE	HERE'S WHY
Addicted Like crack	A fan of Excellent Delicious	While talk of addiction is appropriate in some contexts, referring to it casually can cause harm to those who are in fact experiencing addiction, are in recovery, or have friends or relatives who have experienced addiction.

LESS INCLUSIVE	MORE INCLUSIVE	HERE'S WHY
Starving I'm broke	I'm hungry I'm low on cash	These noninclusive phrases are examples of exaggerations. They show disregard and disrespect for individuals experiencing actual crises and real situations of hardship like poverty or hunger. Avoid overstating the seriousness of what you're experiencing.
War/At war War zone Battle Go to war	Hostile environment Difficult Confrontation Dispute Get after it Go get 'em	Use business language in business settings; avoid descriptions of the battlefield. Evoking images of armed conflict and tragedy in the workplace can feel emotional for veterans and survivors of war.

HANDBOOK EXERCISES

THERE'S A WORD FOR THAT

For each of these exaggerations, craft a realistic statement that doesn't overstate the experience.

1. The news of the merger hit the board members like a nuclear bomb.
2. If that customer doesn't renew his contract, he needs to have his head examined.
3. The grand opening was so crowded, they must have been giving away drugs.

_____

_____

_____

THE CONTEXT QUIZ

Make your best guess!

1. What percentage of the US population has served in the military? _____
2. What percentage of adults in the United States have dealt with problematic drug use? _____
3. What percentage of people in the United States are food insecure (meaning that they lack reliable access to a sufficient amount of affordable, nutritious food)? _____

IMAGINE THIS

Your company is about to make a major, long-term investment to enter a new geographic market. The demographics are different from other markets you've served. In the area, there is a major military base, multiple senior-living communities, and a large migrant worker population. How would you go about learning more about the community? What would be the ideal makeup of your regional team in terms of their life experience?

_____

_____

_____

UPON REFLECTION

Have you ever made a misstep in business because you didn't fully understand the life experiences of the colleagues or customers you were interacting with? What happened? What would you do differently if you could do it over again? Write down your thoughts in brief bullet points.

_____

_____

_____

THERE'S A WORD FOR THAT—SAMPLE ANSWERS

1. The Board Members were surprised by the news of the merger.
2. If the customer doesn't renew, we need to work even harder to show them the benefits.
3. They must have been giving super deals for the grand opening event to be so popular.

THE CONTEXT QUIZ—ANSWERS

1. In 2018, about 7% of US adults were veterans, down from 18% in 1980.[60]
2. About 10% of adults in the United States have had drug-use disorder at some time in their lives.[61]
3. According to data from the US Department of Agriculture (USDA), 10.5% (13.8 million) of US households were food insecure at some time during 2020, which was unchanged from 10.5% in 2019.[62]

Additional Words and Phrases to Avoid. The following table is intended to provide a glimpse into the complex etymologies of many common expressions. Although it would be impossible to include an exhaustive list of English phrases with discriminatory histories, this sampling illustrates that many of the terms often used in casual conversation stem from a harmful and discriminatory past.

Each of these familiar phrases has a complex, storied, and troubling history. Some reveal a cultural history of exclusion and contempt. Others have been used to mock or diminish the value of a person or a particular ethnic group.

Using these expressions could be interpreted as a microaggression and quietly undermine the inclusive language you have worked so hard to learn and practice. Avoid these expressions and others like them. Use universal phrases instead. Always be thoughtful about the imagery your words convey. Keep practicing and keep learning.

If you come across other expressions and aren't sure what they really mean, look them up online. Inclusive language means rejecting these kinds of phrases and using words that are more intentional, literal, and aware.

LESS INCLUSIVE	MORE INCLUSIVE	HERE'S WHY
Basket case	Nervous	This term has a negative historic meaning. It originally referred to a person, usually a soldier from World War I, who had lost all four limbs and was carried in a basket.
Cakewalk Takes the cake	That was easy	The *cakewalk* was a processional partner dance frequently performed by enslaved people on plantation grounds, and baked goods were awarded as prizes. The cakewalk was appropriated by performers in racist nineteenth-century minstrel shows, where Black people were portrayed as trying to dance like White people.
Ghetto Barrio	Use the official name of the neighborhood you are referring to.	These terms have long histories but eventually came to indicate any socially segregated, non-White, urban neighborhood.

LESS INCLUSIVE	MORE INCLUSIVE	HERE'S WHY
Grandfathered	legacy, exempted, excused, preapproved, preauthorized	This term has racist origins. It stems from a provision in several southern state constitutions that was designed to enfranchise White people from lower socioeconomic origins, while simultaneously disenfranchising Black people by waiving stringent voting requirements for anyone who was a descendant of a man who had already voted before 1867.
Gyp/Gip Gypsy	Use Romani to refer to a person of Romani descent Use cheat to refer to a person who is dishonest.	This expression most likely evolved as a shortened version of gypsy, a person who should correctly be referred to as *Romani* instead. The Romani are a traditionally nomadic ethnic group that likely originated in India and, today, live mostly in Europe and the Americas. They have been subject to persecution throughout the centuries including enslavement, forced assimilation, and extermination in the Holocaust. The expression "gyp" has become synonymous with cheating someone and should not be used.
Long time no see	I haven't seen you in a long time.	Originally used to mock Native Americans or Chinese pidgin English.
No can do	I can't do it.	Originally a way to mock Chinese people who were learning English.
Paddy wagon	Police car	The term *Paddy* originated in the late 1700s as a shortened form of Patrick and, later, a pejorative term for any Irish person.
Peanut gallery	Crowd Audience	This phrase usually refers to ill-informed hecklers or critics. In reality, the peanut gallery identified a section in theaters, usually the cheapest and least desirable seats, where many Black people had to sit during the vaudeville era.

LESS INCLUSIVE	MORE INCLUSIVE	HERE'S WHY
Powwow	Use only if referring to an Indigenous tribal powwow Meeting or get-together, if referring to any gatherings outside Indigenous culture	This term is only appropriate if you are referring to an actual Native American powwow, which is a sacred gathering or ceremony involving one or more tribes. Applying the term as a verb ("let's powwow") or using it to describe a business meeting or social gathering outside the Native American culture is inappropriate.
Rule of thumb	General rule Standard	This expression has been said to have been derived from an English law that allowed a man to beat his wife with any stick so long as it was no thicker than his thumb.
Sold down the river	Betrayed	During slavery in the United States, enslaved people were often sold and resold by being sent progressively farther down the Mississippi River to plantations where conditions were much harsher.
Tribe Spirit animal	Friends Network Team	It's appropriate to use the term *tribe* if you are referring to an actual Native American tribe. Otherwise, this term can be seen as an appropriation of Native American culture, especially in the United States. Referencing a spirit animal is also an appropriation of Native American culture and should be avoided.

SPECIFIC INDUSTRY GUIDANCE

Healthcare

Why Inclusive Language Is Relevant to Healthcare

Inclusive, effective communication is especially critical to the delivery of quality care. Developing trusting, empathetic relationships that enable open and honest communication leads to more effective treatment. To meet this challenge, providers need to educate and explain treatment plans clearly, protect confidentiality, and ensure they communicate in a way that's culturally appropriate. To feel safe and capable, people need healthcare environments that are free from stigma and discrimination. Inclusive language plays a key role in helping to make healthcare settings safe spaces.

Word Choices You Can Make to Increase Inclusion

- Avoid the word "patient," which has negative connotations and dehumanizes the person who is using healthcare services. "Patient" comes from the Latin word "to suffer" and implies a passive recipient who exists in unequal relationship to healthcare professionals. Instead, use person-first language, refer to each person by their first and last name, or when necessary to maintain confidentiality, consider simply "person" or "client" instead. For instance, you might say "the client in room 211" or "the people in the waiting room."[63]

- Keep this type of person-centered language at the very center of your word choice. For instance, not everyone who is pregnant will identify with the term "mother," so you should say "the pregnant person" instead. Other inclusive replacements include "people with a prostate gland" and "people with a cervix," which acknowledge nonbinary and transgender folks who may have reproductive parts that do not align with their gender identity.

- Don't assume a person's gender based on their name, appearance, or biological sex. To avoid misgendering, use the singular they and other gender-free terms.
- When first meeting someone, state your name, role, and pronouns. Ask what name they would like to be called and which pronouns they use, then thank them for their reply.
- Avoid complicated terms and jargon. Explain all medical terms in simple language, including those that may seem commonplace to you and your team. Many people will not feel comfortable asking for clarification or definition of terms they do not understand.
- Remember that people from different cultures may explain symptoms differently.
- Stay sensitive to the fact that those whom you are caring for may have fears and communication challenges. Poor prior treatment, a mental health issue, or side effects from medication or disease may make connecting, articulating issues, and committing to follow-through difficult for them.
- Unconscious bias training is critical to understanding and mitigating preconceptions about gender, ethnicity, cultural background, physicality, religion, and more, which may interfere with your ability to objectively examine and treat people.

What Else Can You Do?

Can you think of additional examples that may make certain people or groups feel minimized, belittled, silenced, or excluded? In the left column, write those down. Then, on the right, describe a new, inclusive language choice that you think would be better.

_____	_____
_____	_____
_____	_____
_____	_____

A Voice from the Field

As I began to practice inclusive language, I started to ask myself: Am I specifying something that doesn't need to be specified? Is my language accidentally excluding or othering people?

When my wife and I were in the hospital after the birth of our first child, we were in awe of this new person, and having a similar experience to other folks in the labor and delivery unit that day. Then the paperwork started to come in: birth certificate, insurance forms, FMLA, TDI, etc.

We saw forms that said "mother" and "father" that assumed mother had a maiden name, and that auto-entered Mr. next to "father," none of which applied to us (as same-sex cisgender females utilizing cryo-bank sperm). In the pile of all these forms, we saw one form that really did it well: it had "Guardian 1" and "Guardian 2" as optional; it had different genders specified that could be selected on either, and only one section was required. I thought "Wow, they really thought this out." Then I looked at the title of the form and saw "Same-Sex Couple Use Only." I instantly hung my head.

They were so close to getting it right! Why did this form have to only be for same-sex couples? Would heterosexual couples be offended by entering Father and Mother on their own? And what about single parents? What about grandparents or adoptive or transitioning parents that would function as guardian? Imagine the people who created the form, who had to make two forms and go through all of the policy rigamarole of a massive healthcare organization to get two forms, instead of one, approved.

What about the poor administrator who had to determine which form to hand out based on visual assumptions? How many more forms would they need to create and update as other situations came up? All when they could have included almost any other situation with one form for all. Not only is inclusive language supportive of the typical "others"; it is often easier, cheaper, and clearer for everyone.

—**Dallas M. Star, Regional Director, BAYADA Home Health Care**

Real Estate

Why Inclusive Language Is Relevant to Real Estate

Effective communication is essential for real estate agents to develop strong, trusting, and positive working relationships with their clients and to expand their market reach. Real estate is also subject to many federal laws that ensure fairness, including the Civil Rights Act, the Fair Housing Act, the Americans with Disabilities Act, the Equal Credit Opportunity Act, and additional state and local laws.[64] These requirements intensify the need to consistently use language that is thoughtful, inclusive, and without bias.

Word Choices You Can Make to Increase Inclusion

- When introducing yourself, give your name and pronouns, and ask clients for their own. For example, "Hi, I'm Robin. I use he/him pronouns. May I ask your pronouns?"

- Avoid using titles like Mr. or Mrs. or letter salutations such as Dear Sir and Dear Madam. Instead, refer to each person by their full name or first name, if that is what they prefer.
- As a general rule, use the term "partner" instead of "wife," "husband," or "spouse."
- Avoid descriptors that refer to gender, such as "his and her" closets. Substitute the term "dual" at showings and in home listings.
- Eliminate male-centric terms such as "bachelor pad" and "man cave." These terms exclude all other genders. Instead of referring to the "master suite" or "master bedroom," substitute the terms "ensuite bedroom," or "primary bedroom."
- In property listings, avoid expressions such as "perfect for newlyweds" or "ideal to start a family," which exclude many individuals and couples who are not married, are experiencing infertility, or do not intend to have children.
- Keep in mind that many US homebuyers have immigrated to this country. For some, English may not be a first language and they may not feel comfortable. Expressly avoid jargon and cultural expressions (also called idioms) that could be confusing or misleading, for example, "this investment is as good as gold." Instead, use language that's literal and direct.

What Else Can You Do?

Can you think of additional examples that may make certain people or groups feel minimized, belittled, silenced, or excluded? In the left column, write those down. Then, on the right, describe a new, inclusive language choice that you think would be better.

_____   _____
_____   _____
_____   _____
_____   _____

A Voice from the Field

The language we use in regard to the listings, I think that's where we need to be particularly sensitive right now. "Family room" is usually rejected in our MLS (Multiple Listing Service), so we are prohibited from using that, but in my conversations with colleagues, we thought that we should also avoid things like "master bedroom." We use "ensuite bedroom" or "primary bedroom" instead.

—Colleen Blondell, Real Estate Agent and Board Member, NC Board of Realtors

Government and Public Services

Why Inclusive Language Is Relevant to Government and Public Services

On January 20, 2021, President Biden's first day in office, he signed an executive order declaring that "affirmatively advancing equity, civil rights, racial justice, and equal opportunity is the responsibility of the whole of our Government." On June 25, the president issued an "Executive Order on Diversity, Equity, Inclusion, and Accessibility (DEIA) in the Federal Workforce."[65] It calls for the federal government, as the nation's largest employer, to cultivate a workforce that draws from the full diversity of the United States and to be a model for DEIA: a place where all employees are treated with dignity and respect. The order also noted that "a growing body of evidence demonstrates that diverse, equitable, inclusive, and accessible workplaces yield higher-performing organizations."

By practicing inclusive language, government employees, whether at the federal, state, or local level, can actively support the intent, aspiration, and fulfillment of these policies.

Word Choices You Can Make to Increase Inclusion

- Use singular they and other gender-free words instead of binary terms like "men and women" or "ladies and gentlemen."
- Name your pronouns in email signatures and when meeting people for the first time. By doing so, you normalize the practice and encourage others to do the same. When meeting someone, say "May I ask your pronouns?"
- Use racial, national, ethnic, and religious descriptors only as adjectives, not nouns. For instance, say "people who are Hispanic" or "people who are Muslim" instead of "Hispanics" or "Muslims."
- Pay attention to your language choices regarding disability, invisible illness, mental health, and neurodiversity.
- Follow all guidelines for gender-free language in the US Congress, as outlined by the federal government in 2021. Some examples include replacing:
  - himself and herself with themselves;
  - chairman with chair;
  - mother, father, daughter, son, sister, and brother with terms such as parent, child, and sibling;
  - his or her and he or she with relevant descriptors such as member or delegate.[66]

- Learn and practice the United Nations' "Guidelines for Gender-Inclusive Language in English," designed to ensure that language is nondiscriminatory and makes gender visible only when it is relevant to the communication.[67]

What Else Can You Do?

Can you think of additional examples that may make certain people or groups feel minimized, belittled, silenced, or excluded? In the left column, write those down. Then, on the right, describe a new, inclusive language choice that you think would be better.

A Voice from the Field

In both private and public spaces, words matter. We must continue to advocate for authentic inclusion and allyship. By encouraging inclusive language, we prioritize inclusive action and aim to serve our community with a foundation of dignity and respect. From pronouns to personal ideologies, I strive to respect peoples' perspectives. The willingness to learn, unlearn, and advocate will get us far and make us fluent in the love language of inclusion.
—**Commissioner Shinica Thomas, Wake County Board of Commissioners**

Education

Why Inclusive Language Is Relevant to Education

Respectful language helps build rapport in classrooms and establishes a positive learning environment where students feel welcome and valued. In brief, it helps create places where students can experience the psychological safety that is necessary for real learning. Respectful language leads to more respectful interactions in classrooms and helps diffuse disciplinary situations. It also acknowledges and increases students' awareness of the complexity of individual identity, creating more respectful discourse among students and with school staff.

Word Choices You Can Make to Increase Inclusion

- At the start of the year, ask students one-on-one what name they would like to be called and which personal pronouns they use. For very young children, you may need to ask parents and guardians instead. Misgendering is far too common in education. Never assume a person's gender identity based on their name or appearance.

- Greet students daily as "students," instead of "boys and girls."
- Only use descriptors that are truly relevant. For instance, you don't need to say "the girl in the sandbox" or "the young man in the wheelchair" when both "girl" and "young man" could easily be replaced with "student," "child." This rule also applies to race and ethnicity. Note how often you may be referring to people by their race and gender when such descriptors are irrelevant and unnecessary. Could you say "the person in the yellow shorts" or the "the math teacher with the brown hair" instead?
- Refer to school breaks by their seasonal names (e.g., "winter break," not "Christmas break").
- Insist on—and teach—person-first language and the singular "they." Share the specific terms included in this book to teach students how they can appropriately refer to classmates and staff from different backgrounds and with diverse identities.
- Teach students about neurodiversity, emphasizing the wide range of natural human cognitive processing and thinking styles.
- Reject all language that relies on "norms" and "normality." Remember there is no such thing as normal.
- If a student uses an offensive term, don't ignore it. Instead, thoughtfully explain why the term or expression is not respectful, suggest an alternative, ask them to apologize thoughtfully, then move on. If the behavior is persistent, you may need to implement repercussions.
- When speaking to a class, keep in mind that the life experiences of some students may not be shared by all. Start by saying "For those of you who _____" (for example, live with a grandparent or have visited another state) to remove stigmas that make some students feel excluded.

What Else Can You Do?

Can you think of additional examples that may make certain people or groups feel minimized, belittled, silenced, or excluded? In the left column, write those down. Then, on the right, describe a new, inclusive language choice that you think would be better.

_____	_____
_____	_____
_____	_____
_____	_____

A Voice from the Field

My daughters have had several challenging experiences when educators did not prac-tice inclusive language. They've often heard "the Black girl over there" and been called out by an elective teacher for being the "only Black girl signed up for the class." My girls and I have many conversations about what it feels like to be excluded and how important it is not to hurt others simply by using casual language that does not include everyone. Raising teenagers right now has caused me to think before I speak. It's a work in progress.

And, as I am learning to implement inclusive language into my whole life, I realized how often I use the term "guys" when addressing a whole class of students—like "hey guys, let's line up" or greeting students with "hi guys"—until being told by a student that she wasn't a guy. That was a learning experience for me.

—**Angela Dawson, Principal, Raleigh Oak Charter School**

Finance and Insurance Services

Why Inclusive Language Is Relevant to Finance and Insurance

The finance and insurance industries operate at the nexus of three forces that make inclusive language a high priority: diversity, trust, and compliance. These two indus-tries serve people of all backgrounds in virtually every segment of our diverse society. Additionally, finance and insurance professionals must conduct themselves according to a thorough and complex set of legal requirements. To effectively handle clients' personal and professional financial and insurance matters, trusting relationships are paramount. Communicating clearly and inclusively is key to serving a diverse client base and expand-ing your capabilities.

Word Choices You Can Make to Increase Inclusion

- Be mindful of the imagery in your language. Replace "black market," "white list," and "sanity check" with "illegal market," "allow list," and "confidence check" respectively.
- Reject binary terms for gender. Use singular they and gender-free terms instead.
- Avoid accidental ageism by removing culturally exclusive phrases like "you can't teach an old dog new tricks" and "young at heart." When referring to age or generation, use

those descriptors as adjectives instead of nouns, such as in "our baby boomer clients" and "people from younger generations."

- Use plain language to make your messages easily understood by the broadest range of people. Avoid acronyms, jargon, cliches, and colloquialisms that are geographically or culturally specific, as in "piece of cake" or "knock on wood."
- Take the time to explain all necessary industry-specific terms in simple language, including those that may seem commonplace to you and your team. Many people will not feel comfortable asking for clarification or definition of terms they do not understand.
- Rely on person-centered phrases that acknowledge the fullness of personal identity, and never use racial, ethnic, religious, or socioeconomic descriptors as nouns. For instance, say "people who are affluent" and "people from lower socioeconomic origins."
- Certain numbers have negative connotations in some cultures. For example, the number 4 in Chinese and Japanese cultures is considered unlucky because it's associated with death; a seemingly friendly and upbeat slogan like "Here 4 You" would be inappropriate.
- Consistently integrate translations, subtitles, and voiceovers into your communications to facilitate understanding for customers and colleagues who have hearing or vision difficulties.
- Remember that English may not be a first language for many customers. When hiring suppliers, check to see if they have expertise in language inclusion.
- Use the word "diverse" as an adjective, for example, a "diverse team" or "diverse workplace." Don't use it to describe a single person; an individual is not diverse. For example, replace "I'm going to interview a diverse candidate" with "This candidate would add to the diversity of my team."

What Else Can You Do?

Can you think of additional examples that may make certain people or groups feel minimized, belittled, silenced, or excluded? In the left column, write those down. Then, on the right, describe a new, inclusive language choice that you think would be better.

_____   _____

_____   _____

_____   _____

_____   _____

A Voice from the Field

The concept of inclusive language has been one of the more powerful lessons learned on my personal DEI journey. Although I had initially focused on the conversational aspect of inclusive language, I quickly found that it's just as important to also assess areas that we engage with in our daily lives (partnerships, systems, processes, tools).

This was evident when a colleague pointed out that our financial reporting was using gender-biased terminology (workman's compensation insurance vs. worker's compensation insurance). It was a valuable lesson in realizing that it's very easy to overlook items that have been in place for some time, and just as easy to take corrective action when applying the right lens of inclusivity.

—**Brian Pressler, CFO, BAYADA Home Health Care**

Retail

Why Inclusive Language Is Relevant in the Retail Sector

Whether in a physical or online store, the retail experience centers on direct interaction with customers. The most successful retailers know that the products they sell, where they sell them, who does the selling, and how they advertise must all be designed with diversity and inclusion in mind. Word choice is an essential element of this mix. Ideally, the words that customers read and hear will make them feel welcome and empowered.

Language also helps to positively differentiate the customer experience of one retailer versus its competitors. In short, it helps you reach a bigger market and build loyal customer relationships. From the customer point of view, many of today's shoppers are guided by DEI-related values. As the US population becomes increasingly diverse and intersectional, a growing number of consumers are choosing to shop with retailers that acknowledge their personal identities and actively support social causes that promote diversity, equity, inclusion, and accessibility.

Word Choices You Can Make to Increase Inclusion

- To avoid misgendering your customers, avoid all gender-specific greetings, such as "ladies and gentlemen," and use "everyone" or "you all" instead.
- Examine your product descriptions and personal language choices for bias about the end-consumer. Men wear makeup and nail polish. Women use grills and play

video games. LGBTQ+ couples create wedding registries and buy matching sets of pajamas, coffee mugs, and so much more. Using gender-free terms not only makes all people feel welcome and included, but also expands your market reach.

- Avoid culturally specific figures of speech that customers who don't speak English may find difficult to understand.
- Always explain terms like "out of stock, "back ordered," and "contactless payment" that may feel commonplace to you, but might leave your customers confused and feeling excluded.
- Insist on digital accessibility for your website, mobile app, and any other digital systems, processes, or tools. Test your content using the Flesch–Kincaid readability test to make sure customers of all reading levels are included.[68]
- Pay attention to the words you're using to describe other people's bodies, like "plus size" "junior," and "skinny mirror" and work toward more body-positive terminology that rejects the idea of some bodies being "normal" and others being abnormal.

What Else Can You Do?

Can you think of additional examples that may make certain people or groups feel minimized, belittled, silenced, or excluded? In the left column, write those down. Then, on the right, describe a new, inclusive language choice that you think would be better.

_____	_____
_____	_____
_____	_____
_____	_____

A Voice from the Field

Retail is about welcoming people and making them feel they want to be part of your business. The primary way we welcome people is grounded in the language we use, so getting educated on inclusive language is a game changer for retailers.

Customer experience and service are the only real competitive advantages for online or store-based brands. I have been amazed at the range of opportunities for increasing inclusivity in retail once you start examining it with an educated eye.

—Phil Kowalczyk; Former President, COO, and CEO; The Body Shop, Talbots, J. Jill, and The Robert Allen Group

Manufacturing

Why Inclusive Language Is Relevant to Manufacturing

Great manufacturing requires great teamwork. A diverse group of frontline professionals needs to accept, respect, trust, and communicate effectively with each other in order to do their best work. Frontline employees are the force that drives results at manufacturing companies. It's up to these workers to ensure that operations run smoothly, that quality products are made to exact specifications, and that those products reach customers on schedule. Disengaged employees drag down results, but effective, inclusive communication can play a key role in engaging and motivating employees, increasing productivity and making everyone feel valued, empowered, and encouraged to participate as part of the team.

Word Choices You Can Make to Increase Inclusion

- With a predominantly male workforce, the manufacturing sector should pay special attention to male-centric terms that exclude all other genders, like "manpower," "man hours," "mankind," "tradesman," and "foreman." Instead, use genderless terms like "humanpower," "labor hours," "humankind," "skilled professional," and "supervisor."
- Never refer to a woman over 18 years old as a "girl," which is patronizing and condescending. Similarly, avoid "young lady," "kiddo," "young man," "whiz kid," and "rookie."
- Use racial, ethnic, religious, and other identity descriptors only as adjectives, never as nouns. For instance, say "our Latine workforce," "people who identify as LGBTQ+," and "people with disabilities."
- Teach the difference between—and inclusive language for—sex, gender, and sexual orientation.
- Remove stigmas around mental health, invisible illness, disabilities, and neurodiversity by practicing and insisting on person-first language that starts, most typically, as "a person with."
- Remember, you only need to mention identity descriptors when they are relevant to the current conversation. Most of the time, identity descriptors about race, ethnicity, gender, and more can be omitted entirely. For instance, you might refer to a coworker as "Casey, the machinist with long, brown hair."
- When you don't know the most respectful way to refer to someone, it's usually okay to ask. Say "Could I ask your ethnicity so I can be sure I'm using the most inclusive language?"

What Else Can You Do?

Can you think of additional examples that may make certain people or groups feel minimized, belittled, silenced, or excluded? In the left column, write those down. Then, on the right, describe a new, inclusive language choice that you think would be better.

_____	_____
_____	_____
_____	_____
_____	_____

A Voice from the Field

We can't be our best at Boeing without every teammate participating fully at work. And yet, sometimes anxieties or other roadblocks can cause a person to hold back. We're trying to change that by focusing on three habits as a team: seeking, speaking, and listening. We are committed to seeking out the places where things aren't going well, so we can address issues before they become problems; to getting all perspectives on the table, so every team member feels safe to speak up; and to listen to one another openly, so people are heard. [. . .]

Each of us has a role to play in making our workplace more inclusive. For me, I hold myself accountable by making sure I am always seeking new perspectives. I'll often notice that in a meeting, there's somebody who's quiet and I'll ask, "What are you thinking?" On many occasions, that simple question has resulted in hearing a great idea that wouldn't be on the table otherwise.

—**Michael D'Ambrose, Executive Vice President and CHRO, Boeing**

Service and Hospitality

Why Inclusive Language Is Relevant to the Service and Hospitality Industries

The service and hospitality industries rely on customer relationships and trust. To differentiate themselves from competitors, these businesses must create and market a superior customer experience that connects the consumer with the brand. Inclusive language is a key element of the guest experience. And research proves that when brands invest in creating inclusive experiences, consumers reward them with long-term loyalty.

Word Choices You Can Make to Increase Inclusion

- Adopt gender-free language. As an example, on flights and in airports, you could easily remove the phrase "ladies and gentlemen" and simply ask "for the attention of all passengers."
- Describe families with all-inclusive terms. For example, replace "mom and dad" with "the grown-ups," "adults," or another neutral term. This shift makes sure you're including LGBTQ+ families, families with single parents, and stepparents.
- As a general rule, use "partner" instead of "husband" or "wife." For instance, when making a restaurant reservation for a couple that you know is celebrating an anniversary, you might say "congratulations to you and your partner" or "we look forward to celebrating with both of you."
- Make your online interactions as genuine and personalized as your in-person conversations. While keeping your replies to emails and social media comments on-brand, simultaneously strengthen your relationship with every customer by letting them know they're talking with a person who respects them—not a machine.
- Never assume someone's gender based on their name, voice, appearance, or more. Avoid "ma'am" and "sir," referring to people by their first name—or full name—instead.
- In kitchens, reconsider terms like "shotgun" and "fire," which carry connotations of violence.
- When interacting with new customers by phone or email, consider including the phrase "please let us know if you require any assistance or reasonable accommodations, and we will be happy to provide them." Statements like these make it clear that you are both willing and prepared to accommodate people with disabilities.

What Else Can You Do?

Can you think of additional examples that may make certain people or groups feel minimized, belittled, silenced, or excluded? In the left column, write those down. Then, on the right, describe a new, inclusive language choice that you think would be better.

_____	_____
_____	_____
_____	_____
_____	_____

A Voice from the Field

The service industry provides an interesting environment for consideration and imple-mentation of inclusive language. On one hand, the culture of kitchens and bakeries has historically skewed toward irreverence and competition. However, over the past few years especially, I've noticed that people from younger generations who are filling most service industry jobs have a more nuanced and diplomatic view of the world, and they really do want to work in collaboration, as a team. As owners and managers, it's our responsibility to cultivate an environment that reflects this shift so that our crews feel comfortable putting in their best work.

—Joshua Bellamy, Baker/Miller/Owner, Boulted Bread

Technology

Why Inclusive Language Is Relevant to the Technology Sector

The technology industry has a perception problem. In addition to being seen as ageist, overly White, and overly male, technology companies are also facing strong distrust from the general public. In fact, according to a 2018 survey by First Round Capital, 77% of tech startup founders agreed with the statement that "tech giants like Facebook, Twitter, Amazon, and Google, are being perceived as evil for taking advantage of our deepest, darkest secrets and fears."[69] While inclusive language is just one part of moving forward, it is a great first step for technology organizations that genuinely want to improve workplace culture, increase productivity, and regain trust.

Word Choices You Can Make to Increase Inclusion

- Directly confront ageism in the industry by removing age-coded language from your job descriptions and interrupting age-related microaggressions—like "okay Boomer" or "you probably haven't heard of this"—whenever you encounter them. Phrases like "digital native," "youthful," "tech-savvy," "recent graduate," and even "entry-level" or "energetic" exclude workers from older generations and lead to a skewed, unrepresentative workforce.
- Insist on digital accessibility and inclusive language for all users. Avoid the words impaired or impairment. For example, substitute "person who uses a screen reader" for "vision impaired" and say "a person who is Deaf or hard of hearing" instead of "hearing impaired."

- Replace tech terms and metaphors that have noninclusive connotations. Change "black hat" to "unethical hacker"; "native" to "built-in"; "webmaster" to "web product owner"; "whitelist" to "safelist"; and "master/slave" with "primary/replica," "primary/standby," or "primary/secondary."
- Use inclusive examples with diverse names, family structures, and more.
- Avoid using idioms, complicated terminology, and jargon that can exclude people who don't have specialized knowledge or who may not be from your same culture.
- With a predominantly male workforce, the tech sector should also pay attention to male-centric terms that exclude all other genders, like "man hours." Instead, use genderless terms like "engineer hours" or "hours of effort."

What Else Can You Do?

Can you think of additional examples that may make certain people or groups feel minimized, belittled, silenced, or excluded? In the left column, write those down. Then, on the right, describe a new, inclusive language choice that you think would be better.

_____	_____
_____	_____
_____	_____
_____	_____

A Voice from the Field

I am a big proponent of eliminating language that indicates ageism in our hiring practices and overall company culture in general. For instance, I always recommend that we don't use language like "junior developer" or "junior project manager," whether it is in our job postings or internal to how we introduce team members. It serves no positive reason, so why do we do it?

On the other side, we as an industry should also strongly consider doing away with "senior" this or that. By default, we are implying anyone who isn't senior is thus junior. Lots of opportunities for growth in inclusive language, but these, to me, get abused way too often and have been in use for far too long.

—Greg Boone, Co-CEO, Blue Acorn iCi

REVIEW, REFLECTION, AND NEXT STEPS

FINAL HANDBOOK EXERCISES

Complete these final handbook exercises to review and reinforce key concepts you have learned.

SAY THIS, NOT THAT
Replace each negative expression below with an inclusive alternative:

Ladies and gentlemen	_____
You guys	_____
OCD	_____
Go to war	_____
Crazy/insane	_____
Preferred pronouns	_____
The homeless	_____
Uppity	_____
"Sold down the river"	_____
Disabled/handicapped	_____
Rule of thumb	_____
Basket case	_____

REVIEW QUIZ
    1. Which of these is NOT one of the Six Guidelines for Inclusive Language?

        a. Put people first.

    b. Be thoughtful about the imagery you use.

    c. Refer to a theoretical person as "he or she."

    d. Use universal phrases.

2. Which of the following best defines inclusive language?

    a. Inclusive language is the new form of political correctness.

    b. Inclusive language means being polite and not offending people.

    c. Inclusive language relates to workplace compliance.

    d. Inclusive language is the daily practice of intentional and unbiased word selection that conveys respect to all people.

3. Which of these expressions does NOT show best practice for inclusive language?

    a. Normal person

    b. Neurodivergent

    c. What are your pronouns?

    d. Person who is Deaf

4. Imagine you are talking with a colleague who uses leg braces. Which of the following is best practice for inclusive language?

    a. Handicapped person

    b. Disabled person

    c. Person who suffers from a disability

    d. I would ask the person what descriptors they use for themselves.

SAY THIS, NOT THAT: SAMPLE ANSWERS

Ladies and gentlemen	Everyone
You guys	You all/Y'all/Folks/Everyone
OCD	Organized/tidy
Go to war	Go after it
Crazy/insane	Wild/surprising
Preferred pronouns	Pronouns
The homeless	A person who is experiencing homelessness
Uppity	Conceited, arrogant, stuck up
"Sold down the river"	Betrayed
Disabled/handicapped	Person with a disability
Rule of thumb	Guideline
Basket case	Nervous/stressed out

REVIEW QUIZ: ANSWERS

1. (c) As a reminder, the six guidelines for inclusive language are:
   a. Put people first.
   b. Use universal phrases.
   c. Recognize the impact of mental health language.
   d. Use genderless language.
   e. Be thoughtful about the imagery you use.
   f. Clarify if you aren't sure.
2. (d) Inclusive language is the daily practice of intentional and unbiased word selection that conveys respect to all people.
3. (a) There is no "normal"; people are people in all our diversity.
4. (d) Ask people what descriptors they use to identify themselves; mirror their language.

Personal Reflection

Think about each of the following three questions. Write down three bullet-point answers for each one:

1. What are the three most valuable concepts or insights you have learned from this handbook?
   - _____
   - _____
   - _____

2. How do you think you can apply what you have learned to how you personally communicate at work?
   - _____
   - _____
   - _____

3. What are three ways you can help to promote the practice of inclusive language in your workplace?
   - _____
   - _____
   - _____

Closing Thoughts

Inclusive language is the cornerstone of an inclusive workplace culture. It activates the power of diversity and builds the foundation for a fair and equitable work environment. By drawing your attention to your own linguistic patterns and moving forward with intentional, unbiased language, you can speak to every member of the audience, respect each team member's individual perspective, and seek to understand the complexities of human identity. You also set the foundation for a more productive, collaborative, enjoyable work environment.

It is easy to notice blatant racism, sexism, or discrimination. It is much harder to examine our own unconscious biases, in-groups, out-groups, and deep-seated, potentially harmful, patterns of language. Real change requires work. Congratulations on starting that work by reading this handbook and completing the exercises. You've successfully taken the critical first steps and now have a strong foundation to build on.

As you begin your inclusive language practice, remember that inclusion is an ongoing commitment, not an achievement. Inclusion requires us to keep learning, practicing, and pressing forward.

You won't get everything right, but if you keep trying, you will make progress. Remember that the first steps are always the hardest and **practice makes progress, not perfection.** Along the way, we know you'll find that the tangible benefits of diversity, equity, and inclusion—like increased productivity, better problem-solving, creativity, innovation, employee retention, and an open, equitable culture—are absolutely worth the effort.

SUPPLEMENTARY INFORMATION

Key Terms

Acquired Diversity Traits you gain from experience, such as cultural fluency or military training.

African A native or inhabitant of Africa; a person of African descent.

African American An American with partial or total ancestry from Africa.

Afro-Caribbean A person of African descent living in or coming from the Caribbean.

Agender Not identifying with any given gender.

Ally Refers to someone who shows solidarity with a specific underrepresented or historically marginalized community. Being an active ally is an ongoing and active process through which someone who has privilege chooses to stand for—and with—marginalized or underrepresented communities by taking actions to dismantle systems of oppression.

Alzheimer's Disease A progressive disease that impairs memory and other cognitive functions.

Ancestry A person's genetic descent.

Anti-Semitism Prejudice against people who are Jewish.

Asexual Describes a lack of sexual attraction. People who are asexual may desire emotionally or romantically intimate relationships but have little interest in sex.

Asian A native or inhabitant of Asia; a person of Asian descent.

Asian American An American who is of Asian descent.

Attention Deficit Hyperactivity Disorder (ADHD) A chronic condition with symptoms that might include difficulty focusing, restlessness, fidgeting, and impulsiveness. People with ADHD often also display traits like creativity, hyperfocus, curiosity, and entrepreneurship.

Autism Spectrum Disorder (ASD) A developmental condition that encompasses a broad range of characteristics that can include difficulty communicating, behavior issues, obsessive interests, repetitive behaviors, and difficulty with social interaction. People with this diagnosis might also show exceptional attention to detail, memory, creativity, and tenacity.

Bias Disproportionate weight in favor of or against a person, idea, or thing, usually in a way that is closed-minded, prejudicial, or unfair.

Bigender A gender identity in which someone identifies with two genders, such as male *and* female, or as two other gender identities.

Binary Something that has two parts. In this context, it is used to describe the delineation of sex or gender into two distinct and opposite forms: male and female; man and woman.

Bisexual Refers to someone who is sexually attracted to more than one gender. This often means being attracted to both men and women (the traditional binary genders)—hence the "bi-" prefix.

Black Black is a term that encompasses people whose ancestors descend from the African diaspora.

Cisgender A person whose gender identity corresponds with the sex they were assigned at birth.

Cultural Diversity The existence of a variety of cultural or ethnic groups within a society.

Cultural Identity A part of a person's identity, related to nationality, ethnicity, religion, social class, generation, locality, or any other social group that has its own distinct customs, values, or heritage.

Dementia A group of conditions characterized by an impairment of at least two brain functions, such as memory loss or impaired reasoning.

Demisexual Refers to people who experience sexual attraction only after establishing an emotional or romantic relationship with someone.

Diaspora A scattered population of people who have settled far from their ancestral homelands.

Diversity The understanding and acceptance of the fact that people have individual characteristics, which make them unique from each other, particularly when comparing individuals in a group.

Diversity, Equity, and Inclusion (DEI) As defined by Inclusion Hub, the symbiotic relationship, philosophy, and culture of acknowledging, embracing, supporting, and accepting those of all racial, sexual, gender, religious, and socioeconomic backgrounds, among other differentiators.

Down Syndrome A genetic disorder characterized by developmental delays, intellectual disabilities, and a range of physical disabilities.

Ethnicity A social group identity that centers mostly around shared language and culture.

Equity Fairness and justness, recognizing that we do not all start from the same place.

Gay Refers to a person who is attracted to someone of the same gender.

Gender Refers to social constructs and identities. Therefore, it is self-defined, nonbinary, and can be malleable, changeable, or even fluid.

Gender Fluid A gender identity that varies over time.

Gender Queer Not identifying with the man/woman binary or rejecting any one specific identity. This is also sometimes used as an umbrella term for many non-cisgender identities.

Gender Variant Not conforming to gender-based expectations of society.

Heterosexual An identity in which a person is attracted to people of the opposite sex.

Inclusion Refers to a cultural and environmental feeling of belonging assessed as the extent to which people are valued, respected, accepted, and encouraged to fully participate.

Inclusive Language The daily practice of intentional and unbiased word selection that acknowledges diversity, conveys respect to all people, and promotes equitable opportunities.

Indigenous Descriptor for a group of people who are native to a specific region.

Inherent Diversity Traits you are born with, which is widely described as gender, ethnicity, and sexual orientation.

Intellectual and Developmental Disabilities (IDD) This term describes many severe, chronic conditions that are due to mental and/or physical impairments. People who have IDD might have problems with language, mobility, learning, or independent living.

Intersectionality The unique combinations of ways that people belong to multiple social categories at the same time, including race, class, gender, and sexual orientation.

Intersex A general term used for a variety of conditions in which a person is born with a reproductive or sexual anatomy that doesn't seem to fit the typical definitions of female or male.

Invisible Disability A disability that is not immediately apparent to others. The term is often interchangeable with invisible illness.

Invisible Illness A medical condition and diagnosis that impacts a person's life but is not immediately apparent to other people. The term is often used interchangeably with invisible disability, however not all invisible illnesses will be referred to as disabilities by the person with the diagnosis.

Latino, Latina, Latine A person of Latin American descent. Latino is used to refer to a man of Latin American descent; Latina is used to refer to a woman of Latin American descent; Latine is a gender-neutral description of anyone of Latin American descent.

Lesbian A term for women who are attracted to women. Some women who are attracted to women prefer the terms gay or queer instead.

LGBT The original acronym for the LGBTQIAP+ community, standing for lesbian, gay, bisexual, and transgender.

LGBTQIAP+ Acronym for lesbian, gay, bisexual, transgender, queer/questioning, intersex, asexual/aromantic, and pansexual communities. The plus sign represents other non-heteronormative identities not included in the acronym.

Little Person/Little People People having an adult height under 147 centimeters (4 feet, 10 inches).

Microaggressions The casual, frequent, unintentional, and often unconscious insults and indignities referring to a person's identity.

Misgender A common microaggression in which a person does not use a person's affirming name, pronouns, and honorifics.

Nationality Refers to the country or countries that a person might consider their home.

Native American Any person indigenous to North, Central, or South America, especially used to refer to folks indigenous to the United States.

Neurodiversity The concept that all neurological differences are to be recognized and respected as any other human variation. These differences can include those labeled with dyspraxia, dyslexia, attention deficit hyperactivity disorder, dyscalculia, autism spectrum disorder, Tourette syndrome, and others.

Nonbinary Refers to someone who rejects or does not identify with the gender binary of man or woman. A person may identify as both man and woman simultaneously, in fluctuation, as something else entirely, or as no gender at all.

Obsessive-Compulsive Disorder Obsessive-compulsive disorder (OCD) is characterized by intrusive thoughts and fears (obsessions) that lead to compulsive behaviors. OCD often centers on themes such as a fear of germs or the need to arrange objects in a specific manner. Symptoms usually begin gradually and vary throughout life.

Pansexual Refers to people whose attraction to folks does not depend on gender identity.

Personal Identity The unique identity of a person based on the characteristics they feel attached to.

Person of Color Any person who is not White.

Physicality Relating to the body, especially one's appearance.

Post-Traumatic Stress Disorder Post-traumatic stress disorder (PTSD) is a condition in which a person has difficulty recovering after experiencing or witnessing a terrifying event. The condition may last months or years, with triggers that can bring back memories of the trauma accompanied by intense emotional and physical reactions.

Pronouns A word that can function by itself as a noun and that refers either to the participants in the conversation (I, you) or to someone or something mentioned elsewhere (she, he, they).

Queer An umbrella term for sexual and gender identities that are not heterosexual or are not cisgender. This term may also be used by people who reject the notion of labels.

Questioning Refers to someone who is currently questioning their sexual identity, gender identity, gender expression, or some combination of the three, and might be in the process of exploration.

Race Refers to a mix of physical, behavioral, and cultural attributes.

Sex A person's biological features or anatomy. Sex is typically, but not always, classified as binary: female or male.

Sexual Orientation Refers to sexual and/or romantic attraction and includes identities such as heterosexual, gay, lesbian, bisexual, queer, asexual, and more.

Singular "They" "They" as a singular pronoun—a more inclusive term than the clunky and binary "he or she."

Stereotype An overgeneralized belief about a particular category of people; an expectation that people might have about every person in a particular group.

Transgender Refers to individuals whose gender identity does not match the sex that they were assigned at birth.

Two-Spirit Refers to Indigenous peoples who identify as having both masculine and feminine spirits. Two-Spirit is considered a separate, third gender in some Indigenous communities, although the term used to describe a Two-Spirit individual is specific to certain tribes.[70] For example, Nádleehí for the Navajo tribe and Lhamana for the Zuni tribe.

Unconscious Bias Also known as implicit bias, refers to the attitudes or stereotypes that affect our understanding, actions, and decisions in an unconscious manner.

Workplace Incivility Low-intensity deviant workplace behavior with ambiguous intent to harm the target. For example, being rude, gossiping, interrupting, or mocking.

Works Referenced

[1] "Calculating the Cost of Employee Turnover." G&A Partners, June 3, 2018.

[2] "Fostering Innovation Through a Diverse Workforce." *Forbes Insights*, 2011.

[3] "Racial Equity in Financial Services." McKinsey and Company, September 10, 2020.

[4] "Delivering Through Diversity." McKinsey and Company, January 18, 2018.

[5] "How Diverse Leadership Teams Boost Innovation." Boston Consulting Group, January 23, 2018.

[6] "Hacking Diversity with Inclusive Decision Making." Cloverpop, 2017.

[7] Otto, Nick. "Avoidable Turnover Costing Employers Big." *Benefit News*, August 9, 2017.

[8] "Workplace Communication Statistics (2021)." Pumble, 2021.

[9] "Communicating in the Modern Workplace: How Millennials and Their Managers Compare." Queens University Online, 2022.

[10] "21 Collaboration Statistics That Show the Power of Teamwork." Bit.AI Blog, 2020.

[11] Harrell, Jason. "Employees Stay When They Are . . ." LinkedIn, April 29, 2015.

[12] Laker, Benjamin. "Culture Is a Company's Single Most Powerful Advantage. Here's Why." *Forbes*, April 23, 2021.

[13] Jackson, Amy Elisa. "New Study: 3 in 5 U.S. Employees Have Witnessed or Experienced Discrimination." Glassdoor, July 22, 2020.

[14] "The Cost of Racial Injustice." Society for Human Resource Management, May 24, 2021.

[15] Lloyd, Camille. "One in Four Black Workers Report Discrimination at Work." Gallup, January 12, 2021.

[16] "Infographic: Persistence of Racial Discrimination in U.S. Hiring." Northwestern University, September 13, 2017.

[17] "Women in the Workplace 2021." McKinsey and Company, September 27, 2021.

[18] "Women in the Workplace: The State of Women Hangs in the Balance." McKinsey and Company, November 16, 2021.

[19] Kolmar, Chris. "Age Discrimination Statistics 2022." Zippia, August 31, 2021.

[20] "LGBT People's Experiences of Workplace Discrimination and Harassment." Williams Institute, UCLA, September 2021.

[21] Ecklund, Elaine Howard. "Examining the Effects of Exposure to Religion in the Workplace on Perceptions of Religious Discrimination." Rice University, 2016.

[22] Krentz, Matt, Justin Dean, and Gabrielle Novacek. "Diversity Is Just the First Step. Inclusion Comes Next." Boston Consulting Group, April 24, 2019.

[23] Reiners, Bailey. "57 Diversity in the Workplace Statistics You Should Know." Built In, February 25, 2022.

[24] Gurchiek, Kathy. "Report: Most Companies Are 'Going Through the Motions' of DE&I." Society for Human Resource Management, February 23, 2021.

[25] "Inclusive Mobility: How Mobilizing a Diverse Workforce Can Drive Business Performance." Deloitte, 2018.

[26] "Intersex People." Office of the High Commissioner of Human Rights, United Nations, 2022.

[27] Jones, Jeffrey M. "LGBT Identification in U.S. Ticks up to 7.1%." Gallup, February 17, 2022.

[28] Ibid.

[29] "Disability Impacts All of Us." U.S. Centers for Disease Control and Prevention, September 16, 2020; "Chronic Diseases in America." U.S. Centers for Disease Control and Prevention, January 24, 2022.

[30] Smith, S. E. "Why I Say 'Disabled Person' Instead of 'Person With Disabilities.'" Rewire Newsgroup, September 14, 2016.

[31] "Invisible Disabilities: List and General Information." *Disabled World*, August 15, 2021.

[32] Pulrang, Andrew. "8 Disability Podcasts That Are Well Worth a Listen." *Forbes*, June 26, 2021.

[33] "Bringing Visibility to Invisible Disabilities and Invisible Illness." Invisible Disabilities Association. YouTube, December 3, 2017.

[34] "New 'Make It Work' Employment Empowerment Video Series." World Institute on Disability, November 6, 2019.

[35] "Disability Language Style Guide." National Center on Disability and Journalism, August 2021.

[36] "About Intellectual and Developmental Disabilities (IDDs)." National Institutes of Health, November 9, 2021.

[37] "Podcasts." Neurodiversity Network, October 2020.

[38] "About Learning Disabilities." LD Online, February 2022.

[39] Siperstein, Gary N., Robin C. Parker, and Max Drascher. "National Snapshot of Adults with Intellectual Disabilities in the Labor Force." *Journal of Vocational Rehabilitation*, 2013.

[40] "100 Words to Describe Coworkers (And Why You Should Use Them)." Indeed, February 17, 2022.

[41] Porath, Christine, and Christine Pearson. "The Price of Incivility." *Harvard Business Review Magazine*, January–February 2013.

[42] Leasca, Stacey. "10 Body-Positivity Podcasts to Download for a Boost of Self-Love." *Real Simple*, March 30, 2021.

[43] Umoh, Ruth. "Study Finds You're Less Likely to Get Hired if You're Overweight. Here's How to Avoid This Bias." CNBC, November 3, 2017.

[44] Warner, Jennifer. "Height May Make or Break Your Career." WebMD, October 17, 2003.

[45] "Basic Facts About Dwarfism." Understanding Dwarfism, February 2022.

[46] Bryce, Emma. "What's the Difference Between Race and Ethnicity?" Live Science, February 8, 2020.

[47] Chou, Vivian. "How Science and Genetics Are Reshaping the Race Debate of the 21st Century." Harvard University Graduate School of Arts and Sciences, April 17, 2017.

[48] Crochet, Evan. "Let's Nix Latinx: Latine Is the Word You Were Already Looking For." The Diversity Movement, January 18, 2022.

[49] "Top 10+ Diversity Videos." Ongig, August 18, 2020.

[50] *Latino USA* podcast, 2022.

[51] Goode, Justine. "10 Essential Podcasts from AAPI Creators." *Vanity Fair*, April 2, 2021.

[52] "Indigenous People in the United States." International Work Group for Indigenous Affairs, February 2022.

[53] "Foreign-Born Workers Made Up 17.4 Percent of Labor Force in 2019." U.S. Bureau of Labor Statistics, May 29, 2020.

[54] "About Three-in-Ten U.S. Adults Are Now Religiously Unaffiliated." Pew Research Center, December 14, 2021.

[55] "Style Guide—The Name of the Church." The Church of Jesus Christ of Latter-day Saints, April 13, 2021.

[56] "Employment Law: Religious Discrimination in the Workplace." LawShelf. YouTube, May 22, 2020.

57 Lankford, James and Russell Moore. "The Real Meaning of the Separation of Church and State." *Time*, January 16, 2018.

58 Alidina, Raafi-Karim. "3 Ways to Build a Religiously Inclusive Work Culture." Human Resource Executive, January 18, 2020.

59 "List of Religious Populations." Wikipedia, February 2022.

60 Schaeffer, Katherine. "The Changing Face of America's Veteran Population." Pew Research Center, April 5, 2021.

61 "10 Percent of US Adults Have Drug Use Disorder at Some Point in Their Lives." National Institutes for Health, November 18, 2015.

62 Food Security in the U.S.: Key Statistics and Graphics." Economic Research Service. U.S. Department of Agriculture, September 8, 2021.

63 Neuberger, Julie. "Let's Do Away with 'Patients'." *British Medical Journal* (BMJ), June 26, 1999.

64 "What Everyone Should Know About Equal Opportunity Housing." National Association of Realtors, February 2022.

65 "Executive Order on Diversity, Equity, Inclusion, and Accessibility in the Federal Workforce." The White House, June 25, 2021.

66 "The U.S. Congress' New Gender Neutral Language [14 terms are a no-no]." Ongig, January 12, 2021.

67 "Guidelines for Gender-Inclusive Language in English." The United Nations, February 2022.

68 "Flesch–Kincaid Readability Test Tool." WebFX, February 2022.

69 "State of Startups 2018." First Round Capital, 2018.

70 Matthews-Hartwell, Terra. "LGBTQ2S Advocacy, and Nativeout." Indian Health Service, February 2022.

Acknowledgments

Thank you to Susan Unger for her thoughtful input and partnership in bringing this book to market, and to our content and marketing team for their detailed edits and high standards for excellence, including Bob Batchelor, Kaela Sosa, Amber Keister, Allison Bennett, and Evan Crochet. The many steps involved in creating this book would have been significantly less enjoyable without each of you.

Thank you also to every one of our past, present, and future colleagues at The Diversity Movement—the people with whom we get to practice and learn about inclusive language every day—including Kurt Merriweather, Kristie Davis, Jamie Ousterout, Shelley Willingham, Susie Silver, Melanie Sanders, Michelle Perez, Adriane Edge, Angela Scipio, Sharon Delaney-McCloud, and so many more.

A special thank you to The Diversity Movement's CEO, Donald Thompson, for persistently urging us to write this book and for providing meaningful direction in naming and promoting this work; to Brad Norr for cover design; to Debra Nichols for copy editing; and to Kyle Sarofeen at Hamilcar Publications who partnered with us through the publication process.

To all the people from our personal and professional lives and client organizations who contributed their voices, inclusive language dilemmas, and uncomfortable word choice questions to make this book even better—including Laura Wahl, Kristen Koba-Burdt, Sue Tomcyzk, Dallas Star, Colleen Blondell, Shinica Thomas, Angela Dawson, Brian Pressler, Phil Kowalczyk, Michael D'Ambrose, Joshua Bellamy, and Greg Boone—we are grateful.

To the amazing people who are actively supporting our mission—our partners, clients, and especially our board members and investors—thank you. You are helping us reach, educate, and inspire people all over the world to create cultures of inclusion and belonging.

We are continually inspired and supported by our families, most especially our husbands, Don and Josh, and our mothers, Dianne and Carol.

Part of what this long list of helpful people proves is exactly what we tell our clients: diversity, equity, and inclusion lead to better decision-making, better problem-solving, and measurably better outcomes. A cross-functional team of diverse people with diverse skill sets, areas of expertise, and life experiences made this book better than it ever could have been if only the two of us had shaped it.

Thank you all.

About the Authors

JACKIE FERGUSON is Head of Content and Programming and co-founder of The Diversity Movement. Known globally for its groundbreaking diversity, equity, and inclusion (DEI) programming that drives real-world business results, the company was named to *Inc.* magazine's 2021 Best in Business List in DE&I Advocacy. Ferguson, a Certified Diversity Expert (CDE), oversees a team of writers, editors, and visual storytellers that create industry-leading content, as well as world-class educational and digital learning resources.

A noted writer and subject matter expert, Ferguson hosts *Diversity: Beyond the Checkbox*, a podcast rated as one of the Top 10 diversity podcasts to follow globally. She is a member of the Forbes Business Council, National Diversity Council, and is published in *Forbes*, Almanac, and other publications. Ferguson is an in-demand keynote speaker on diversity and belonging topics. She is an alumna of the University of South Florida and lives in North Carolina with her husband and daughter.

ROXANNE BELLAMY, CDE, is Managing Editor at The Diversity Movement, ensuring that the company's world-class content is accurate, actionable, and trustworthy. She believes words shape reality. A writer's job, especially regarding DEI, is to put the best words in the best order to shape the best reality. A recognized thought leader, Bellamy's work centers on contributing with integrity to the ever-evolving conversation around diversity, equity, and inclusion and workplace culture.

A graduate of UNC–Chapel Hill and Cambridge University, Bellamy studied English, linguistics, and anthropology. In her earlier career, she worked as a writer across several industries, including retail, manufacturing, craft beer, education, and hospitality. Bellamy is also a mother, wife, sister, daughter, and athlete.

the diversity movement

The Diversity Movement offers employee experience applications that personalizes diversity, equity, and inclusion (DEI) for your organization and delivers real-world business outcomes. Our productized DEI journey is built on digital learning tools, world-class content, conversational AI, and analytics. A key offering is the MicroVideos by The Diversity Movement library, a learning platform created to scale DEI learning across the organization. *Fast Company* named MicroVideos as one of its 2022 World Changing Ideas, among just forty-two honored globally in the workplace category. DEI Navigator is a subscription-based model that enables small- and midsized organizations to scale their DEI journey for their organizations. The Diversity Movement powers scalable and sustainable workplace excellence via a data-driven approach focused on business results.

Data-Driven | Technology-Enabled | DEI Expertise
Learn more at www.thediversitymovement.com

CPSIA information can be obtained
at www.ICGtesting.com
Printed in the USA
JSHW060055310523
42404JS00002B/159